Thomas Ray Eaton

Shakespeare and the Bible

Thomas Ray Eaton

Shakespeare and the Bible

ISBN/EAN: 9783337413620

Printed in Europe, USA, Canada, Australia, Japan

Cover: Foto ©Thomas Meinert / pixelio.de

More available books at **www.hansebooks.com**

SHAKESPEARE

AND

THE BIBLE:

SHOWING HOW MUCH THE GREAT DRAMATIST WAS
INDEBTED TO HOLY WRIT FOR HIS PROFOUND
KNOWLEDGE OF HUMAN NATURE.

BY

REV. T. R. EATON, M.A.,

OF CORPUS CHRISTI COLLEGE, CAMBRIDGE,

(WHO DEDICATES THIS WORK, WITH FILIAL REGARD, TO HIS FATHER.)

Third Thousand.

LONDON:
JAMES BLACKWOOD, PATERNOSTER ROW.

CONTENTS.

	Page
INTRODUCTORY REMARKS	9
A Quotation from Richard III.	13
,, ,, Henry VIII.	14

CHAPTER I.
Parallels from Macbeth and King John 16

CHAPTER II.
Play—King John 18

CHAPTER III.
Play—Macbeth 22

CHAPTER V.
Play—Hamlet 26
A passage from Henry V. 30
Two from Richard III. 31

CHAPTER VI.
Play—Richard III. 34

Chapter VII.

Play—Henry VIII. 40

Chapter VIII.

Play—Henry V. 49

Chapter IX.

Play—Henry VI. (Parts I., II., III.) 56

Chapter X.

As You Like It 74

Chapter XI.

Richard II. 75
Example from Henry V. 78

Chapter XII.

Play—Henry IV. (Parts I., II.) 91
An Example from the Two Gentlemen of Verona . 101
„   „   „ As You Like It 102
Play—Merry Wives of Windsor 110
An Example from Henry IV. 115

Chapter XIII.

Play—Troilus and Cressida 117

Chapter XIV.

Play—Anthony and Cleopatra 120
An Example from Merry Wives of Windsor . . . 122

Chapter XV.

Play—Timon of Athens 123

CONTENTS. vii

Page

Chapter XVI.

Coriolanus 125
Cymbeline 126
Play—Julius Cæsar 127
,, Othello 127

Chapter XVII.

Play—Tempest 131
An Example from Midsummer Night's Dream—an
    Example from Macbeth 135
Play—Midsummer Night's Dream 136
,, King Lear 137
,, Romeo and Juliet 138
,, Twelfth Night; or, What you Will 141
Example from Coriolanus 143

Chapter XVIII.

An Example from As You Like It 144

Chapter XIX.

An Example from The Comedy of Errors 145

Chapter XX.

Twelfth Night; or, What You Will 146

Chapter XXI.

Play—Two Gentlemen of Verona 148
,, The Merchant of Venice 150

Chapter XXII.

Play—The Winter's Tale 170

Chapter XXIII.
Play—All's Well that Ends Well 173

Chapter XXIV.
Play—Love's Labour Lost 180
" Much Ado About Nothing 196
" As You Like It 200

Chapter XXV.
Play—Taming of the Shrew 203

Chapter XXVI.
Measure for Measure 205
Example from Midsummer Night's Dream 209

Chapter XXVII.
Play—Comedy of Errors 210
Concluding Remarks of a General Nature 214

SHAKESPEARE AND THE BIBLE.

Introductory Remarks.

LESS is said to be known of Shakespeare than of any other writer who attained equal celebrity during his lifetime. This may be partly owing to the absence of that periodical literature which is now the rapid vehicle of information, and partly to his calling and the nature of his great works, which, however well adapted for the closet, were originally designed for the stage. We need not, therefore, be much surprised that the cravings of curiosity should have been satisfied with gossip and scandal, since there was nothing better to be had. It is now generally admitted that his parents held a respectable position in life, and that he must have had the advantage of a good grammar-school education. The stories of his stealing deer from Sir Thomas Lucy's grounds at Charlecote, and of his holding horses at the door of one of the London theatres, have deservedly fallen into discredit; but it is reasonable to believe that he was indebted to his mother for early lessons of piety, and that he was conversant with the Holy Scriptures from a child. The Reformation could not fail, from the very nature of it, to tinge the literature of the Elizabethan æra. It gave a logical and disputatious character to the age, and produced men mighty in the scriptures. The butcher, the barber, and the baker, were in the habit of chopping logic, each in his own sphere.

Hence we need not wonder that the humour of Shakespeare's clowns is always, more or less, argumentative.

The *argals* of the gravedigger in Hamlet are probably no fictitious corruption of the *ergos* which were then in every body's mouth. This particular consequence of the Reformation served to cramp the genius of Shakespeare, at least to the extent of giving a rough *date* to the period of his writings; the second effect, his profound acquaintance with Holy Writ, on the other hand, assisted to raise them above the trammels of place and time. Before proceeding to the immediate matter in hand, which is to show, by new evidence, the vastness of Shakespeare's Bible lore, it may be well to point out the kind of benefit which he may be fairly supposed to have thence derived.

The Bible professes to make men " wise unto salvation." Such being its end and aim, it is for this purpose a sufficient and infallible rule both of faith and conduct. But since the wisdom here indicated is really a concrete, it follows that the man thus instructed is taught many things. He learns, for instance, the Divine will so far as regards mankind; he acquires such an insight as is absolutely necessary into the mystery of the redemption by the blood of the Saviour; he has a just apprehension of the scope and obligation of moral duty; and he has knowledge to some extent of the change wrought in human nature by original sin. God and man being described as contracting parties in a covenant, it was necessary that their *characters* should be mutually known. God, therefore, has been mercifully pleased to reveal himself as fully as the best and wisest of men can be rendered capable of apprehending him in this state of being, and he has unfolded all the windings of the heart. This last He has done in various ways. Sometimes by direct announcement: sometimes by short and pithy maxims, as in the Book of Proverbs: and generally by dramatic representations of the actions of men of every variety of disposition, and of every grade of life, from the king upon his throne to the shepherd in the field and the captive in the dungeon, who have lived in different ages of the world. This mode of teaching must have had an irresistible charm to one of Shakespeare's peculiar bent. We are all affected in a less lively manner, by being told that " the heart is deceitful above all things," than when the same truth is brought home to us by such exclamations as Nathan's—" Thou art the man;" or by such a fall as Peter's in the denial of his Master, after the strong protestation even, that he would "sooner die." Neither would any homily upon the heroism of self-denial make so lasting an impression upon us, or fire us with so noble an emulation, as the example of David, when he put the water from his parched lips with—"Be it far from me, O Lord, that I should do this : is not this the blood of the men that went in jeopardy of their lives?" (2 Sam. xxiii.) It is pleasant to fancy the delight with which young Shakespeare must have feasted upon these and like divine lessons, unconscious, the while, that he was strengthening his pinions for loftier flights than had ever been attained by uninspired man. It is the prerogative of genius to seem to create what it only receives and reproduces, as the die converts bullion into current coin, or the "bag o' the bee" distils honey from collected sweets. Wisdom in selection and power in reproduction determine the quality of genius. In storing his mind, Shakespeare went first to the word and then to the works of God. In shaping the truths derived from these sources, he obeyed the instinct implanted by Him who had formed him *Shakespeare*. Hence his power of inspiring us with sublime affection for that which is properly good, and of chilling us with horror by his fearful delineations of evil. Shakespeare perpetually reminds us of the Bible; not by direct quotation, indirect allusion, borrowed idioms, or palpable imitation of phrase and style, but by an elevation of thought and simplicity of diction which are not to be found elsewhere. A passage, for instance, rises in our thoughts, unaccompanied by a clear recollection of its origin. Our first impression is, that it *must* belong *either* to the *Bible* or to *Shakespeare*. No other author excites the same feeling in an equal degree. In Shakespeare's plays religion is a vital and active principle, sustaining the good, tormenting the wicked, and influencing the hearts and lives of all. What uninspired writer ever made us feel the value of prayer, as a privilege, so affectingly as Shakespeare has done *in three words?* It flashes across the brain of Othello the Moor—the rough soldier—that possibly his friend may be practising upon him—a conditional curse therefore burst from his lips; "*If* thou dost slander her and torture me, '*Never* PRAY *more!*'"

The mysterious power of religion over bad men is thus displayed in Richard III.:—

"Thus, thus, quoth Forrest, girdling one another
Within their alabaster innocent arms:
Their lips were four red roses on a stalk,
Which, in their summer beauty, kiss'd each other.
A book of prayers on their pillow lay;
Which once, quoth Forrest, almost changed my mind."

The book of prayers—the calm deep sleep—give such mute evidence of innocence and trust in God, as to suspend for an instant the designs of heartless villany. Another instance of the influence of religion on a proud man is found in Cardinal Wolsey, who knows the practical precepts of the gospel, and their value.

THE PLAY OF HENRY VIII.

["So God created man in his own image, in the image of God created he him." Gen. i.]

"Mark but my fall, and that that ruin'd me.
Cromwell, I charge thee, fling away ambition;
By that sin fell the angels, *how can man then,
The image of his Maker,* hope to win by't?
Love thyself last: cherish those hearts that hate thee;

["Do good to them that hate you."—Matt. v. 44.]
["In lowliness of mind *let each esteem other better than themselves.*"—Philippians ii. 3.]

Corruption wins not more than honesty—
Still in thy right hand carry gentle peace,
To silence envious tongues. Be just and fear not:
Let all the ends thou aim'st at be thy country's,
Thy God's, and truth's; then if thou fall'st, O Cromwell,
Thou fall'st a blessed martyr. Serve the king;
And pr'ythee lead me in:
There take an inventory of all I have,
To the last penny; 'tis the king's:
My robe,
And my integrity to heaven, is all

I dare now call mine own. O Cromwell, Cromwell!
* Had I but served my God with half the zeal
I served my king, he would not in mine age
Have left me naked to mine enemies."

Such language from the Cardinal is rendered natural by the time chosen for its utterance. A man of his powerful and cultivated intellect might unbosom himself to a faithful and devoted servant, and denounce the worthlessness of worldly ambition, while smarting under the rod of despotic wrath, and stung by the taunts of merited reproach. We come now to the consideration of parallel passages.

---

* ["Had I but served my God," &c.] This sentence was really uttered by Wolsey.—JOHNSON.

SHAKESPEARE AND THE BIBLE.

CHAPTER I.

THE PLAY OF MACBETH.

ACT IV.　SCENE III.

"*Macduff.* My wife killed too?
Rosse. I've said.
Malcolm. Be comforted:
Let's make us med'cines of our great revenge, to cure this deadly grief.
Macduff. He has no children!"

So Constance speaks to Pandolph in King John—

"*Constance.* He talks to me that never had a son."

And again—

"Had you such a loss as I, I could give better comfort than you do."

So Job—

"I also could speak as ye do: if your soul were in my soul's stead, I could heap up words against you, and shake mine head at you. But I would strengthen you with my mouth, and the moving of my lips should assuage your grief." Job xvi. 4, 5.

CHAPTER II.

THE PLAY OF KING JOHN.

ACT III. SCENE I.

"*Constance.* A wicked day, and not a holy day!
What hath this day deserved, what hath it done;
That it in golden letters should be set
Among the high-tides in the kalendar?
Nay, rather *turn this day out of the week;*
This day of shame, oppression, perjury:
Or, if it must stand still, *let wives with child
Pray that their burdens may not fall this day,*" &c.

Misery wrings from Job a similar malediction; how strictly therefore, in such cases, does Shakespeare keep within the bounds of probability—

"*Let the day perish wherein I was born,* and the night in which it was said, There is a man-child conceived. As for that night, let darkness seize upon it; let it not be joined unto the days of the year, let it not come into the number of the months." Job iii. 3, 6.

The play of King John is indebted to Scripture in several more instances; we will notice these, therefore, before proceeding to other plays.

ACT III. SCENE IV.

"*Constance.* For since *the birth of Cain, the first male child,*
To him that did but yesterday suspire,
There was not such a gracious creature born."

["Birth of Cain, the first male child."]—"And Adam knew his wife; and she conceived and *bare Cain,* and said, I have gotten a man from the Lord." Gen. iv. 1.

Could Constance better express, than by such allusion to Eve's first-born, how much her hopes had anchored upon her child, and how utterly these hopes were shipwrecked?

ACT IV. SCENE III.

HUBERT *and* FAULCONBRIDGE, *the Bastard of* RICHARD I.

"*Hubert.* Do but hear me, sir.
The Bastard. Ha! I'll tell thee what;
Thou art damn'd so black—nay, nothing is so black;
Thou art more deep damn'd than Prince Lucifer:
There is not yet so ugly a fiend of hell
As thou shalt be, if thou didst kill this child."

["More deep damn'd than Prince Lucifer."] "How art thou fallen from heaven, O Lucifer, son of the morning! how art thou cut down to the ground, which didst weaken the nations! Thou *shalt be brought down to hell, to the sides of the pit.*" Isa. xiv. 12—15.

END OF ACT IV. SCENE III.

In the speech of Faulconbridge to Hubert over the remains of Arthur, the king's nephew, there is a passage parallel to a verse in Proverbs: there is also an idea obviously derived from a fact recorded in the 18th chapter of 1 Book of Kings.

"*Faulconbridge.* Go, bear him in thine arms.
I am amazed, methinks; and lose my way
Among the thorns and dangers of this world."

PARALLEL FROM SCRIPTURE.

"Thorns and snares are in the way of the froward: he that doth keep his soul shall be far from them." Prov. xxii. 5.

It is not strange that Faulconbridge should be sometimes lost *among the thorns and dangers of this world,* when we refer to the character of him in

ACT III. SCENE IV.

"*Pandulph.* The bastard Faulconbridge
Is now in England, *ransacking the church,
Offending charity!*
    Faulconbridge. How easy dost thou take all England
        up!
From forth this morsel of dead royalty,

The life, the right, and truth of all this realm
Is fled to heaven; and England now is left
To tug, and scramble, and to part by the teeth
The unowed interest of proud swelling state.
Now for the bare-picked bone of majesty,
Doth dogged war bristle his angry crest,
And snarleth in the gentle eyes of peace:
Now powers from home, and discontents at home,
Meet in one line; and vast confusion waits
[As doth a raven on a sick, fallen beast]
The imminent decay of wrested pomp.
*Now happy he, whose cloak and cincture can
Hold out this tempest."*

"Now happy he," that is, whose mind is fully prepared to surmount these difficulties.

["Cloak and cincture can hold out this tempest."]— "And it came to pass in the meanwhile, *that the heaven was black with clouds and wind,* and there was a great rain. And Ahab rode, and went to Jezreel.

"And the hand of the Lord was on Elijah; and he *girded up his loins, and ran before Ahab to the entrance of Jezreel.*" 1 Kings xviii. 45, 46.

The Oriental custom of girding the loins, as Elijah does in the instance before us, is used metaphorically here, as it is in 1 Peter i. 13—

"Wherefore gird up the loins of your mind."

The play of Macbeth may be reproduced, and the play of Hamlet examined, before plays composed of English history are again referred to.

CHAPTER III.

THE PLAY OF MACBETH.

ACT I. SCENE II.

"*King Duncan.* Dismay'd not this our captains, Macbeth and Banquo?
Soldier. Yes;
As sparrows, eagles; or the hare, the lion.
If I say sooth, I must report they were
As cannons overcharg'd with double cracks;
So they
Doubly redoubled strokes upon the foe:
Except they meant to bathe in reeking wounds,
Or memorize another Golgotha,——
I cannot tell." * * * *

["Golgotha."]—"And they bring him unto the place called *Golgotha*, which is, being interpreted, the place of a skull." Mark xv. 22.

ACT II.   SCENE III.

Enter a PORTER.

"*Porter.* Here's a knocking, indeed! If a man were porter of hell-gate, he should have old turning the key. Knock, knock, knock! Who's there, i' the name of *Belzebub?*"

["Belzebub."]—Shakespeare is indebted for this word to the New Testament: in the present instance, perhaps, without being aware of it, or at least without a thought of detection, from 11th chapter of St. Luke:—

"*Knock,* and it shall be opened unto you.
To him that knocketh, it shall be opened."
"He casteth out devils through *Beelzebub.*"

v. 9, 10, 15.

That the words *Knock* and *Beelzebub* should be found in the 11th chapter of Luke, thus near each other, and should be thus connected by Shakespeare, is too strange to escape notice.

ACT II.   SCENE III.

When the Murder of KING DUNCAN *is first discovered.*

"*Macduff.* O horror! horror! horror! Tongue, nor heart,
Cannot conceive nor name thee!
Macbeth and Lennox.   What's the matter?

Macd. Confusion now hath made his masterpiece! Most sacrilegious murder hath broke ope
The Lord's anointed temple, and stole thence
The life o' the building."

Several extracts from the Bible that denounce regicide shall be produced, in which King Saul is called "*The Lord's anointed.*"

["The Lord's anointed."]—"And David said to Abishai, Destroy him not : for who can stretch forth his hand against *the Lord's anointed,* and be guiltless?" 1 Sam. xxvi. 9.

"The Lord forbid that I should stretch forth mine hand against *the Lord's anointed.*" 1 Sam. xxvi. 11.

"This thing is not good that thou hast done. As the Lord liveth, *ye are worthy to die,* because ye have not kept your master, *the Lord's anointed.*" 1 Sam. xxvi. 16.

["Lord's anointed *temple.*"]—The additional word *temple* may have been supplied by expressions which were used by Him whom the Jews crucified—

"Destroy this *temple,* and in three days I will raise it up." John ii. 19.

"When he spake of the *temple* of his body." John ii. 21.

Again,

ACT II.   SCENE III.

"*Banquo.* Fears and scruples shake us :
In the great hand of God I stand; and thence
Against the undivulg'd pretence I fight
Of treasonous malice."

["Hand of God."]—"Thou hast also given me the shield of thy salvation : *and thy right hand hath holden me up.*"   Psalm xviii. 35.

Banquo confesses that he is innocent of Duncan's murder; but he hints that he strongly suspects the one who puts him to death.

ACT V.   SCENE V.

"*Macbeth.* And all our yesterdays have lighted fools the way *to dusty death.*"

"*The dust of death*" is to be met with in the 22nd Psalm.   Dusty death alludes to the sentence pronounced against Adam—

"Dust thou art, and unto dust shalt thou return."

The sentence that almost directly follows the one just noticed,

"*Life's but a walking shadow,*"

is very similar to an expression in Psalm xxxix. 6,

"Man walketh in a vain shadow."

c

CHAPTER V.

THE PLAY OF HAMLET, PRINCE OF DENMARK.

ACT I. SCENE I.

"*Horatio.* A mote it is to trouble the mind's eye."

THIS idea is evidently taken from these words, "Why beholdest thou the mote that is in thy brother's eye?" They are to be found in the 7th chapter of St. Matthew.

ACT II. SCENE II.

"*Hamlet.* O Jephthah,* judge of Israel—what a treasure hadst thou!
Polonius. What a treasure had he, my lord?
Hamlet. Why—*one fair daughter, and no more,* the which he loved passing well."

---

* A ballad, " Jeffa, Judge of Israel," is said to be here quoted by Hamlet: the remark may be correct—yet a writer unversed in Holy Writ would never thus recur to such a subject in a ballad.

Polonius. Still on my daughter.
Hamlet. Am I not i' the right, *old Jephthah?*
Polonius. If you call me *Jephthah,* my lord, I have a daughter that I love passing well."

["O Jephthah, *judge of Israel.*"]—It is stated that Jephthah judged Israel six years. Judges xii. 7.

[" One fair daughter."]—"And Jephthah vowed a vow unto the Lord, and said, If thou shalt without fail deliver the children of Ammon into mine hands, then it shall be, that whatsoever cometh forth of the doors of my house to meet me, when I return in peace from the children of Ammon, shall surely be the Lord's, and I will offer it up for a burnt-offering.

" So Jephthah passed over unto the children of Ammon to fight against them; and the Lord delivered them into his hands.

" And Jephthah came to Mizpeh unto his house, and, behold, *his daughter* came out to meet him with timbrels and with dances : *and she was his only child; beside her he had neither son nor daughter.* And it came to pass, when he saw her, that he rent his clothes, and said, Alas, my daughter! thou hast brought me very low, and thou art one of them that trouble me : for I have opened my mouth unto the Lord, and I cannot go back.

" And he sent her away for two months.

" And it came to pass, at the end of two months, that she returned unto her father, who did with her according to the vow that he had vowed." Judges xi. 30, to end of 39.

Hamlet detects the object Polonius has in view; and seems to hint that Polonius will as thoroughly ruin the prospects of Ophelia by his present folly, as Jephthah did those of his daughter by a rash vow.

ACT III.   SCENE IV.

The next extract is from the conference which Hamlet has with his mother relative to her marriage with his uncle—the murderer of the late king.

"*Hamlet.*   Look you now, what follows:
Here *is* your husband; *like a mildew'd ear,*
Blasting his wholesome brother."

This alludes, says Steevens, to Pharaoh's dream in Gen. xli.

"And I have dreamed a dream, and there is none that can interpret it: and I have heard say of thee, that thou canst understand a dream to interpret it. * * * "I saw in my dream, and behold, seven *ears came up* in one stalk, *full and good:*

"And behold, seven *ears,* withered, thin, and *blasted* with the east wind, sprung up after them;

"And the *thin ears devoured the seven good ears.*" Gen. xli. 15, 22—24.

ACT V. SCENE I.

A Churchyard. THE CLOWNS *are digging* OPHELIA'S *Grave.*

"1*st Clown.* There is no ancient gentlemen but gardeners, ditchers, and grave-makers; they hold up Adam's profession.

2*nd Clown.* Was he a gentleman?
1*st Clown.* He was the first that *ever bore arms.*
2*nd Clown.* Why, he had none.
1*st Clown.* What, art a heathen? How dost thou understand *the Scripture?* The *Scripture* says, *Adam digged; could he dig without arms?*"

["Adam digged."]—"The Lord God sent him (Adam) forth from the garden of Eden, *to till the ground* from whence he was taken." Gen. iii. 23.

The CLOWN *throws up a Skull.*

"*Hamlet.* That skull had a tongue in it, and could sing once: How the knave *jowls it to the ground,* as if it were *Cain's jawbone,* that did the first murder!"

["Cain's jawbone."]—"And Cain talked with Abel his brother: and it came to pass, when they were in the field, that Cain rose up against Abel his brother, and slew him." Gen. iv. 8.

A bitter comment this on the effect of habit! Hamlet observes, with disgust, that even so sad an office as gravedigging begets in time a shocking disregard for the remains of the dead. In the 3rd act and 3rd scene, allusion is made to the death of Abel, when the king's conscience wrests from him this secret confession of his guilt:—

"*King.* O, my offence is rank, it smells to heaven;
It hath the primal eldest curse upon't:
A brother's murder!"

Shakespeare's knowledge of mankind proved, both directly and indirectly, from Scripture. What light the poet throws upon the dark stratagems of kings to retain and increase power, in the speeches about to be quoted! By these he shows that princes who are ambitious, bold, and wise, are wont to profess an anxiety to maintain in all their actions, especially those of moment, godly honour and Christian benevolence before those who are to be sacrificed, when necessary, for their aggrandizement. Thus Henry V. appears to be influenced by holy counsel from the Archbishop of Canterbury, concerning hostility with France, when, at the same time, he is inwardly resolved to wage war against her—

"*King Henry.* We charge you in the name of God, take heed:
For never two such kingdoms did contend
Without much fall of blood; whose guiltless drops
Are every one a woe—a sore complaint,
'Gainst him whose wrong gives edge unto the swords
That makes such waste in brief mortality.

Under this conjuration speak, my Lord :
For we will hear, note, and believe in heart,
That what you speak is *in your conscience wash'd
As pure as sin with baptism.*"

["Conscience wash'd."]—" Be baptized, and wash away thy sins." Acts xxii. 16.

A Soliloquy of the notorious DUKE OF GLOSTER, *afterwards* RICHARD III.

" *Gloster.* I do the wrong, and first begin to brawl.
The secret mischiefs that I set abroach,
I lay unto the grievous charge of others.
Clarence, whom I indeed have laid in darkness,
I do beweep to many simple gulls,
Namely, to Stanley, Hastings, Buckingham ;
And tell them, 'tis the queen and her allies
That stir the king against the duke my brother :
Now they believe it ; and withal whet me
To be revenged on Rivers, *Dorset,** Gray.
But then I sigh, and with a *piece of Scripture*
Tell them, that *God bids us do good for evil :*
And thus I clothe my naked villainy
With old odd ends, stolen forth of holy writ ;
And seem a saint when most I play the devil."

[" Do good for evil." " Odd ends, stolen forth of Holy Writ."]—" Love your enemies, *bless* them that *curse* you, *do good to them that hate you,* and *pray for them which despitefully use you,* and persecute you." Matt. v. 44.

---

* Some editions of Shakespeare insert *Vaughan* instead of *Dorset.*

Shortly before Gloster's speech in the 1st Act and 3rd Scene of Richard III., Rivers says—

" A virtuous and a christian-like conclusion, *To pray for them that have done scathe to us.*"

" Be not overcome of evil, but *overcome evil with good.*" Rom. xii. 21.

How much the words spoken by Gloster, and those by Henry V. to the Archbishop, remind us of the pithy sentence in the 25th chapter of Proverbs—

"The heaven for height, and the earth for depth, and the heart of kings is unsearchable."

And as Shakespeare has, in many instances, used the Proverbs of Holy Writ, he might, and probably did, derive from these Proverbs no slight knowledge of men as they appear in their several stations, and play their parts in the great and complicated drama of the world. Now genius, thus developed, could draw real characters apparently true to life, yet after its own fancy. And this it does in some instances to the flagrant violation thereby of historical statements. Whether, however, the liberties taken with history, by making men better or worse than they are said to have been when alive, proceeded from a love of exercising such power, or from motives as base, we need not here determine. Quotations from Proverbs we shall soon have occasion to notice particularly.

The soliloquy of the Duke of Gloster admits at least of this additional remark; it well answers the description given in Prov. xxvi., of one whose hatred is cloaked by policy:—

" He that hateth dissembleth with his lips, and layeth up deceit within him; when he speaketh fair, believe him not, for there are seven abominations in his heart."

CHAPTER VI.

THE PLAY OF RICHARD III.

ACT II.   SCENE III.

A Street near the Court.

" 3 *Citizen.*   Neighbours, God speed!

1 *Citizen.*   Give you good-morrow, sir.

3 *Citizen.*   Doth the news hold of good King Edward's death?

2 *Citizen.*   Ay, sir, it is too true; God help the while!

3 *Citizen.*   Then, masters, look to see a troublous world.

1 *Citizen.*   No, no; by God's good grace his son shall reign.

3 *Citizen.   Woe to that land that's govern'd by child !*"

" Woe to thee, O land! when thy king is a child.' Eccles. x. 16 (Steevens).

ACT IV.   SCENE IV.

The widow.of Edward IV. is unable to promote the match desired by Richard III. between himself and his niece Elizabeth: this princess, after her uncle's death, becomes the Queen of Henry VII. By this alliance the houses of York and Lancaster are united, and the Wars of the Roses are henceforth for ever at an end.

"*Queen to Richard.*   Under what title shall I woo
    for thee,
That God, the law, my honour, and her love,
Can make seem pleasing to her tender years?
  Richard. Infer fair England's peace by this alliance.
  Queen. Which she shall purchase with still lasting
    war.
  Richard. Tell her, the king, that may command,
    entreats.
  Queen. That at her hands which *the king's King
    forbids.*"

["King's King forbids."]—"None of you shall approach [i. e., marry] any that is near of kin to him." Lev. xviii. 6.

And amongst the prohibitions stated, we find one equal, in consanguinity, to that of uncle and niece, mentioned in verse 14 of this chapter. The present authorized version of the Bible is the one referred to and quoted, although it was not the version used by Shakespeare. This licence is considered allowable, because passages from our own version are sufficiently like the same passages in all other versions, to show that no mistake can well arise concerning their identity.

ACT I.   SCENE IV.

The Murder of the DUKE OF CLARENCE.

"*Clarence.*   Are you call'd forth from out a world of men,
To slay the innocent ?   *   *   *   *
*   *   *   *   *   *   *
The deed you undertake is *damnable.*"

" *Cursed be he* that taketh reward *to slay an innocent person.*"   Deut. xxvii. 25.

" 1 *Villain.*   What we will do, we do upon command.
2 *Villain.*   And he, that hath commanded, *is our king.*
Clarence.   Erroneous vassal ! the great *King of kings*
Hath in the table of his law commanded,
That *thou shalt do no murder.*"   Exodus xx. 13.

[" King of kings."]   This form of expression is to be found in several parts of the Bible, and of Shakespeare.   We shall direct the reader's attention, for it, to a passage in the 6th chapter of the first Epistle to Timothy :—

———"keep this commandment without spot, unrebukeable, until the appearing of our Lord Jesus Christ:"———"who is the blessed and only *Potentate*, the *King of kings.*" 1 Tim. vi. 14, 15.

Again—

ACT I.   SCENE IV.

"*Clarence.* Tell him (Gloster), when that our
 princely father York
Blest his three sons with his victorious arm,
And charg'd us from his soul to love each other,
He little thought of this divided friendship:
Bid Gloster think on this, and he will weep.
  1 *Villain.* Ay, millstones; as he lesson'd us to weep.
  Clarence. O do not slander him, *for he is kind!*
  1 *Villain. As snow in harvest.* You deceive yourself;
'Tis he that sends us to destroy you here."

["*As snow in harvest.*"]—"As the cold of snow in the time of harvest, so is a faithful messenger to them that send him: for he refresheth the soul of his masters." Prov. xxv. 13.

But before more quotations containing Proverbs are introduced from Shakespeare, observe the clever way in which we are ushered, as it were, into the very apartment in the Tower where the unhappy Clarence is imprisoned; so that we see and hear all that transpires relating to him till the assassins take their departure. Clarence, when first seen, is relating to Brakenbury, lieutenant of the Tower, a *dream* that has been distressing him.

Now what makes the mention of *a dream* worthy of notice here, is *the speech* which falls from the lips of the second villain, as soon as the Duke has been murdered by the first.

"2 *Villain.* A bloody deed, and desperately despatch'd! How fain, like *Pilate*, would I *wash my hands* Of this most grievous guilty murder done!"

There is but one chapter in the New Testament (the 27th of St. Matthew) where we read that

"*Pilate took water, and washed his hands* before the multitude, saying, I am innocent of the blood of this just person."

And *there only* is it stated, that

"Pilate's wife suffered many things *in a dream,* because of him."

The words, therefore, which the second villain utters *relative to Pilate*, seem to conduct us to the *source* whence the *idea of a troubled dream* entered Shakespeare's mind, as a prelude to the horrid event that consigns Clarence to the tomb.

More Proverb-quotations may now be produced, in defence of the conjectures that have been made relating to them.

The following words burst from the lips of the devoted Hastings, a short time before he lays his head upon the block:—

"*Hastings.* O momentary grace of mortal men,
Which we more hunt for than the grace of God!
Who builds his hope in air of your fair looks,
Lives like a (drunken) *sailor on a mast;*
Ready with every nod to tumble down
Into the fatal bowels of the deep."

["Sailor on the mast."]—" Yea, thou shalt be as he *that lieth down in the midst of the sea,* or as he *that lieth upon the top of a mast.*" Prov. xxiii. 34.

The word *drunken,* proves that Shakespeare derived the idea, "lives like a drunken sailor on a mast," from Proverbs, as above indicated.

CHAPTER VII.

THE PLAY OF HENRY VIII.

ACT V.   SCENE II.

Enter the Guard.

"*Cranmer.* For me?
Must I go like a traitor thither?
Gardner. Receive him,
And see him safe i' the Tower.
Cranmer. Stay, good my lords,
I have a little yet to say. Look there, my lords;
By virtue of that ring, I take my cause
Out of the gripes of cruel men, and give it
To a most noble judge, the king my master.
Chamberlain. This is the king's ring.
Surrey. 'Tis no counterfeit.
Suffolk. 'Tis the right ring, by Heaven: I told ye all,
*When we first put this dang'rous stone a rolling,
'Twould fall upon ourselves.*"

["Stone a rolling."]—"*He that rolleth a stone, it will return upon him.*" Prov. xxvi. 27.

As Proverb-quotations cannot again appear thus collectively, passages in the play of Henry VIII., connected with our subject, which have not yet been noticed, may follow in their natural course.

ACT I.   SCENE I.
London.

NORFOLK'S *advice to* BUCKINGHAM, *who plans destruction to* CARDINAL WOLSEY.

"*Norfolk.* Be advised;
Heat not a furnace for your *foe* so hot
That it do singe yourself."

["Furnace for your foe so hot."]—"Then was Nebuchadnezzar full of fury, and the form of his visage was changed against Shadrach, Meshach, and Abednego: therefore he spake, and commanded that they should *heat the furnace one seven times more than it was wont to be heated.*

"Therefore, because the king's command was urgent, and *the furnace exceeding hot*, the *flame of the fire slew* those men that took up Shadrach, Meshach, and Abednego." Dan. iii. 19, 22.

ACT II.   SCENE II.
An Antechamber in the Palace.

From a Dialogue between the LORD CHAMBERLAIN *and the* DUKES OF NORFOLK *and* SUFFOLK, *relative to* CARDINAL WOLSEY.

"*Chamberlain.* Heaven will one day open
The king's eyes, that so long have slept upon
This bold, bad man.

Suffolk. And free us from his slavery.
Norfolk. We had need pray,
And heartily, for our deliverance;
Or this imperious man will work us all
From princes into pages: all men's *honours*
Lie like one lump before him, to be fashion'd
Into what pitch he please."

["Into what pitch."]—This allusion seems to be to the 21st verse of the 9th chapter of the Epistle of St. Paul to the Romans—

"Hath not the potter *power over the clay, of the same lump to make one vessel unto honour, and another unto dishonour?*"—Collins.

We may now add the latter part of Wolsey's speech, which commences with the words—"So farewell to the little good you bear me," in

ACT III. SCENE II.

"*Wolsey.* Vain pomp and glory of the world, I hate ye;
I feel my heart new open'd : O how wretched
Is that poor man that hangs on princes' favours!
There is, betwixt that smile we would aspire to,
That sweet aspect of princes and our ruin,
More pangs and fears than wars or women have;
And when he falls, *he falls like Lucifer,*
Never to hope again."

["Falls like Lucifer."]—" How art thou fallen from heaven, O Lucifer, son of the morning! How art thou cut down to the ground, which didst weaken the nations! For thou hast said in thine heart, I will ascend into heaven, I will exalt my throne above the stars of God: I will sit also upon the mount of the congregation, in the sides of the north :

" I will ascend above the heights of the clouds : I will be like the Most High.

" Yet thou shalt be brought down to hell, to the sides of the pit." Isa. xiv. 12, 13, 14, 15.

ACT V. SCENE I.

"*Cranmer.* I humbly thank your highness;
And am right glad to catch this good occasion
*Most thoroughly to be winnow'd, where my chaff
And corn shall fly asunder:* for, I know,
There's none stands under more calumnious tongues
Than I myself, poor man!"

["Most thoroughly to be winnow'd."]—A turn of expression, not unlike this, occurs in the 9th chapter of the prophet Amos :—

" For lo, I will command, and *I will sift the house of Israel among all nations, like as corn is sifted in a sieve, yet shall not the least grain fall upon the earth.*" Amos ix. 9.

ACT V. SCENE III.

The Palace Yard. Noise and tumult within.
Enter PORTER *and his Man.*

"*Porter.* How got they in, and be hanged?
Man. Alas! I know not; how gets the tide in?
As much as one sound cudgel of four foot
[You see the poor remainder] could distribute,
I made no spare, sir.
Porter. You did nothing, sir.
Man. I am not *Samson,*   *   *   *
* * * * * *   to mow them down before me."

["Samson to mow them down."]—"Then the Philistines said, Who hath done this? (when Samson had, with foxes and firebrands, burnt up their shocks, their standing corn, vineyards, and oliveyards.) And they answered, Samson, the son-in-law of the Timnite, because he had taken his wife, and given her to his companion.

"And the Philistines came up, and burnt her and her father with fire.

"And Samson said unto them, Though ye have done this, yet will I be avenged of you, and after that I will cease.

"And he smote them hip and thigh with a great slaughter." Judges xv. 6—8.

Though this example is given, Shakespeare seems to refer to no particular act of valour performed by Samson; but rather to allude to that quality—*strength*—which rendered him so very remarkable.

The Palace.

The Blessing pronounced by CRANMER, *at the Baptism of the infant Daughter of* ANN BULLEN, *afterwards* QUEEN ELIZABETH.

"*Cranmer.* Let me speak, sir,
For Heaven now bids me ; and the words I utter
Let none think flattery, for they'll find them truth.
This royal infant, (Heaven still move about her!)
Though in her cradle, yet now promises
Upon this land a thousand thousand blessings,
Which time shall bring to ripeness : She shall be
(But few now living can behold that goodness)
A pattern to all princes living with her,
And all that shall succeed : *Sheba was never
More covetous of wisdom and fair virtue,
Than this pure soul shall be:* all princely graces,
That mould up such a mighty piece as this is,
With all the virtues that attend the good,
Shall still be doubled on her : *truth shall nurse her,
Holy and heavenly thoughts still counsel her:*
She shall be lov'd and fear'd : Her own shall bless her :
Her foes shake like a field of beaten corn,
And hang their heads with sorrow : Good grows with her."

As the words—*they shall sit every man under his vine*, &c., are to be found in chap. iv. of Micah, the ideas in italics, *heavenly thoughts*, &c., *foes shake like a field of beaten corn,* &c., may be derived from verses 11, 12, and 13 of this chapter.

In her days, every man shall eat in safety
Under his own vine, what he plants; and *sing*
The merry songs of peace to all his neighbours:
God shall be truly known; and those about her
From her shall read the perfect ways of honour,
And by those claim their greatness, not by blood.
Nor shall this peace sleep with her: but as when
The bird of wonder dies, the maiden phœnix,
Her ashes new create another heir,
As great in admiration as herself;
So shall she leave her blessedness to one
(When Heaven shall call her from this cloud of darkness)
Who, from the sacred ashes of her honour,
Shall star-like rise, as great in fame as she was,
And so stand fix'd: Peace, plenty, love, truth, terror,
That were the servants to this chosen infant,
Shall then be his, and like a vine grow to him;
Wherever the bright sun of heaven shall shine,
His honour, and the greatness of his name
Shall be, and make new nations; he shall flourish,
And, like a mountain cedar, reach his branches
To all the plains about him:—Our children's children
Shall see this, and bless heaven."

"Now also many nations are *gathered against thee,* that say, Let *her be defiled,* and *let our eye look upon Zion.* But they know not the *thoughts of the Lord,* * * * * * for *he shall gather them as the sheaves* into the floor.

"*Arise and thresh, O daughter* of Zion: * * * * * * * *thou shalt beat in pieces* many people." Micah iv. 11, 12, 13.

["*Sheba* was never more covetous of wisdom."] "And when the queen of Sheba heard of the fame of Solomon concerning the name of the Lord, she came to prove him with hard questions.

"And she came to Jerusalem with a very great train, with camels that bare spices, and very much gold and precious stones: and when she was come to Solomon, she communed with him of all that was in her heart. And Solomon told her all her questions: there was not anything hid from the king which he told her not." 1 Kings x. 1—3.

["In her days shall every man eat in safety *under his own vine,* and sing the merry songs of peace."]—Shakespeare might take these ideas from the 1 Book of Kings, iv., or from 1 Book of Maccabees, xiv., as well as, if proof already given be correct, from the prophet Micah.

"Judah and Israel were many, as the sand which is by the sea in multitude, eating and drinking, and making merry.

"And Judah and Israel *dwelt safely, every man under his vine,* and under his fig-tree." 1 Kings iv., 20, 25.

"He made peace in the land, and Israel rejoiced with great joy: *for every man sat under his vine and his fig-tree, and there was none to fray them:*

"Moreover, he strengthened all those of his people that were brought low : the law he searched out ; and every condemner of the law and wicked person he took away." 1 Mac. xiv. 11, 12, 14.

["And make new nations."]—"*And Solomon reigned over all kingdoms,* from the river unto the land of the Philistines, and unto the border of Egypt : *they brought presents, and served Solomon all the days of his life.*" 1 Kings iv. 21.

CHAPTER VIII.

PERTINENT EXTRACTS FROM

THE PLAY OF HENRY V.

ACT I. SCENE I.

THE Archbishop of Canterbury and Bishop of Ely are remarking the great change already visible in the young king since the death of his father.

"*Canterbury.* The king is full of grace and fair regard.
Ely. And a true lover of the holy church.
Canterbury. The courses of his youth promised it not.
The breath no sooner left his father's body,
But that his wildness, mortified in him,
Seem'd to die too : yea, at that very moment,
Consideration like an angel came,
*And whipp'd the offending Adam out of him;
Leaving his body as a paradise,
To envelop and contain celestial spirits.*"

["Like an angel came, and whipped the offending Adam out of him."]—For this figurative mode of expressing a change from sin to godliness, effected by the chastening hand of the Almighty, Shakespeare is indebted to the following extract—

"And the Lord God said, Behold the man is become as one of us, to know good and evil : and now, lest he put forth his hand, and take also of the tree of life, and eat and live for ever: Therefore the Lord God sent him forth from the garden of Eden, to till the ground from whence he was taken. *So he drove out the man; and he placed at the east end of the garden of Eden cherubims*, and a flaming sword which turned every way, to keep the way of the tree of life." Gen. iii. 22—24.

ACT I. SCENE II.

A conference between King Henry and the Archbishop relative to the validity of the Salique law, which is said to be this—

"No woman shall succeed in Salique land :
Which Salique land the French unjustly gloze,"

Says the Archbishop—

" To be the realm of France, and Pharamond
The founder of this law and female bar."

The archbishop then tells the king, that the Salique land is really between the floods of Sala and Elbe, in Germany; that certain French, who settled there, established a law that no female should be an inheritrix in Salique land; and that these French possessed this Salique land 421 years after the death of King Pharamond, who is said to have been the founder of the Salique law.

"*King Henry.* May I, with right and conscience, make this claim?

Canterbury. The sin upon my head, dread sovereign! For in *the book of Numbers is it writ,* When the son dies, let the inheritance Descend unto the daughter."

["Book of Numbers it is writ."]—"And the Lord spake unto Moses, saying, The daughters of Zelophehad speak right : *thou shalt surely give them a possession of an inheritance* among their father's brethren; and *thou shalt cause the inheritance of their father to pass to them.* And thou shalt speak unto the children of Israel, saying, *If a man die and have no son, then ye shall cause his inheritance to pass unto his daughter.*" Num. xxvii. 6—8.

ACT II. SCENE IV.

A turn of expression, remarkably scriptural, occurs in the fourth scene of the second act of Henry V., where Exeter demands, in Henry's name, the crown of France.

Exeter to French king :

"He bids you, *in the bowels of the Lord,* Deliver up the crown."

St. Paul says, too, to Philemon :

"Let me have joy of thee in the Lord : *refresh my bowels in the Lord.*" Epist. to Philemon v. 20.

ACT III. SCENE III.

Harfleur.

The Governor and some Citizens on the Walls: the English Forces below. Enter KING HENRY V. *and his Train.*

The king, in his address to the governor and citizens of Harfleur—which commences with the words,

"How yet resolves the governor of the town?"—

paints, in moving words, the misery which the French must see and suffer, if they again provoke him to attack the town: for then adds the king—

"What rein can hold licentious wickedness,
When down the hill he holds his fierce career?
We may as bootless spend our vain command
Upon the enraged soldiers in their spoil,
As send precepts to the Leviathan
To come ashore. Therefore, you men of Harfleur,
Take pity of your town and of your people,
Whiles yet my soldiers are in my command ;

Whiles yet the cool and temperate wind of grace
O'erblows the filthy and contagious clouds
Of *heady* murder, spoil, and villainy.
If not, why, in a moment, look to see
The blind and bloody soldier with foul hand,
Defile the locks of your shrill-shrieking daughters;
Your fathers taken by the silver beards,
And their most reverend heads dash'd to the walls;
Your naked infants spitted upon pikes:
Whiles *the mad mothers with their howls confus'd*
Do break the clouds, as did the wives of Jewry
At Herod's bloody-hunting slaughtermen."

["As send precepts to the Leviathan to come ashore."]—This seems derived from the 41st chapter of the Book of Job:—

"Canst thou draw out *leviathan* with an hook? or his tongue with a cord which thou lettest down? Will he make many supplications unto thee? Will he speak soft words unto thee? *Will he make a covenant with thee?* wilt thou take him for a servant for ever? None is so fierce that dare stir him up: who then is able to stand before me?" Job xli. 1, 3, 10.

["As did the wives of Jewry at Herod's bloody-hunting slaughtermen."] — These words surely refer to the atrocities committed by Herod the Great when his search for the infant Jesus proved fruitless. Of this slaughter of infants, the following account is given in the 2nd chapter of St. Matthew—

"Then Herod, when he saw that he was mocked of the wise men, was exceeding wroth, and sent forth, *and slew all the children that were in Bethlehem, and in all the coasts thereof, from two years old and under*, according to the time which he had diligently inquired of the wise men. Then was fulfilled that which was spoken by Jeremy the prophet, saying, In Rama was there a voice heard, lamentation, and weeping, and great mourning—Rachel weeping for her children, and would not be comforted, because they are not." Matt. ii. 16, 17, 18.

ACT IV.   SCENE VII.

"*King Henry.* What think you, Captain Fluellen? is it fit this soldier keep his oath?
Fluellen. He is a craven and a villain else, an't please your majesty, in my conscience.
King Henry. It may be, his enemy is a gentleman of great sort, quite from the answer of his degree.
Fluellen. Though he be as goot a gentleman as the tevil is, as *Lucifer and Belzebub* himself, it is necessary, look your grace, that he keep his vow and his oath."

["Lucifer and Belzebub"]—are taken, as we have already shown, from Holy Writ: they are, in the present case, merely the rough expressions of a soldier.

The king's joke is this: he exchanged gloves with Michael Williams, a common soldier, who supposed that the king was a soldier like himself.

They each agree to wear the glove, which each has received from the other, in the bonnet. The soldier then tells the disguised and unknown king, "That if, after to-morrow, he comes to him and says, *This is my glove,* he will take him a box on the ear." The king now traps Fluellen, and sends him with the soldier's glove. The soldier sees his glove in Fluellen's cap, and challenges it with a blow. The king takes care to be present to explain matters, and prevent bloodshed.

ACT IV.   SCENE VIII.

"*King Henry.* O God! thy arm was here,
And not to us, but to Thy arm alone,
Ascribe we all."

PARALLEL IN PSALM XLIV.

"They got not the land in possession by their own sword, *neither did their own arm save them :* but *Thy right hand and thine arm.*" Psalm xliv. 3.

CHAPTER IX.

THE PLAY OF HENRY VI.

THE play of Henry VI., next to the last in historic order, affords several instances of Shakespeare's versatility in the use of Scripture.

PART I. ACT I. SCENE II.

"*Alençon.* Froissart, a countryman of ours, records,
England all Olivers and Rowlands bred,
During the time Edward the Third did reign.
More truly now may this be verified;
For none but *Samsons* and *Goliasses*,
It sendeth forth to skirmish. One to ten!
Lean raw-boned rascals! who would e'er suppose
They had such courage and audacity?"

["For none but Samsons."]—"Samson slew thirty of the Philistines at Ashkelon." Judg. xiv. 19.

Upon another occasion,

"Smote the Philistines hip and thigh with a great slaughter." Judg. xv. 8.

And upon another,

"Slew a thousand men with the jawbone of an ass." Judg. xv. 15.

"He judged Israel in the days of the Philistines twenty years. Judg. xv. 20.

["And Goliasses it sendeth forth to skirmish."]—
"There went out a champion out of the camp of the Philistines, named Goliath, of Gath, whose height was six cubits and a span.

"And the Philistine said, I defy the armies of Israel this day; give me a man, that we may fight together.

"When Saul and all Israel heard those words of the Philistine, they were dismayed, and greatly afraid." 1 Sam. xvii. 4, 10, 11.

["For none but *Samsons* and *Goliasses.*"]— None but men whose exploits astonish and amaze all who know of them; though accounts of them be not exaggerated, like those of the deeds of Oliver and Rowland, Charlemagne's peers, but as veritable as the histories of Samson and Goliath.

ACT I. SCENE II.

"*Charles, Dauphin of France.* Then come o' God's name, I fear no woman.

E

Joan la Pucelle. And, while I live, I'll ne'er fly from a man. (*They fight.*)
Charles. Stay, stay thy hands; thou art an Amazon, And fightest with the *sword of Deborah.*"

["Sword of Deborah."]—This is the celebrated Joan d'Arc, who was burned to death for heresy and magic in the market-place of Rouen. She was servant at a small inn in the village of Domremi, near Vaucouleurs, on the borders of Lorraine, and had been accustomed—till she fancied that she was destined by Heaven to re-establish the throne of France, and thus drew upon her the attention of the French court—to tend the horses of travellers, and to perform other offices commonly allotted to men.

Shakespeare leads us by the word *Deborah* to conceive most exalted ideas of the prowess of this remarkable girl; for facts, related in the subjoined extracts from the book of Judges, directly recur to our memories.

" And *Deborah*, a prophetess, the wife of Lapidoth, she judged Israel at that time. And she sent and called Barak the son of Abinoam out of Kedesh-naphtali, and said unto him, Hath not the Lord God of Israel commanded, saying, Go and draw toward mount Tabor, and take with thee ten thousand men of the children of Naphtali and of the children of Zebulun? *And I will draw unto thee, to the river Kishon, Sisera*, the captain of Jabin's army, *with his chariots and his multitude;* and *I will deliver him into thine hand.*

" And Barak called Zebulun and Naphtali to Kedesh;
and he went up with ten thousand men at his feet:
and *Deborah* went up with him." Judg. iv. 4, 6, 7, 10.

ACT I. SCENE III.

London. The Hill before the Tower.

Enter to Tower Gates, WINCHESTER, *attended.*

CARDINAL BEAUFORT, *Bishop of Winchester, thus addresses the* DUKE OF GLOSTER, *uncle to the King and Protector.*

" *Winchester (great-uncle to the King.)* Nay, stand
    thou back, I will not budge a foot;
This be Damascus, *be thou cursed Cain,*
To slay thy brother, Abel if thou wilt."

An irritating mode this of claiming consanguinity, and at the same time moral superiority, Gloster afterwards acknowledges their relationship. when they renew their quarrel in the first scene of the third act, by the bitter retort—

"Thou bastard of my grandfather!"

[" Cursed Cain."]—" And now art thou (Cain) cursed from the earth, which hath opened her mouth to receive thy brother's blood from thy hand." Gen. iv. 11.

The versatility of Shakespeare is seen in his method of treating the *same facts* from Scripture in various parts of his works; for by them he contrives most vigorously to express either devotion, pride, hatred, levity, authority, or despair.

In the present instance, the mention of Cain's crime is made the most vengeful taunt that a haughty mind can conceive.

ACT II. SCENE I.

Enter TALBOT, BEDFORD, *and* BURGUNDY, *with scaling ladders, &c.*

"*Talbot.* Well, let them practise and converse with
    spirits :
God is our fortress."

The Psalmist's words are,

"The Lord is my rock *and my fortress.*" Psalm xviii. 2.

"Thou art my rock *and my fortress.*" Psalm xxxi. 3.

ACT V. SCENE IV.

Alarum Excursions. Enter JOAN LA PUCELLE.

"*Pucelle.* The regent conquers, and the Frenchmen
    fly.
Now help, *ye charming spells, and periapts ;*
And ye choice spirits that admonish me,
And give me signs of future accidents ! (*Thunder.*)
You speedy helpers, that are substitutes
Under the lordly monarch of the north,
Appear, and aid me in this enterprise !"

["Ye charming spells and periapts."]—"Charms sow'd up. 'Woe to them that sow pillows to all arm-holes, to hunt souls.'" Ezek. xiii. 18.

["Under the lordly monarch of the north."]—The boast of Lucifer in the 14th chapter of Isaiah is said to be, that he "will sit upon the mount of the congregation, in the sides of the north." *Steevens.*

ACT V. SCENE V.

"*York.* Use no entreaty, for it is in vain.
Joan of Arc. Then lead me hence; with whom I
    leave my curse;
May never glorious sun reflex his beams
Upon the country where you make abode!
But *darkness, and the gloomy shade of death*
Environ you."

["Darkness and the gloomy shade of death."]— This expression, says Malone, is scriptural—

"Whereby the day-spring from on high hath visited us, to give light to them *that sit in darkness and in the shadow of death.*" Luke i. 78, 79.

THE PLAY OF HENRY VI.

PART II. ACT I. SCENE III.

QUEEN MARGARET *drops her fan.*

"*Queen Margaret to the Duchess of Gloster.* Give me my fan: What, minion! can you not? I cry you mercy, madam! Was it you?
            (*Gives the Duchess a box on the ear.*)

Duchess of Gloster. Was't I? yea, I it was, proud
Frenchwoman :
Could I come near your beauty with my nails,
I'd set *my ten commandments* in your face."

["Ten commandments."]—The words of the covenant made by the Most High with Moses and with Israel, which are recorded in the 20th Chapter of Exodus, are spoken of in the Old Testament as the *ten commandments*. Thus—"And he (Moses) wrote upon the tables the words of the covenant, the *ten commandments.*" Exod. xxxiv. 28.

We see the use which the angry duchess makes of the words *ten commandments.*

ACT II.   SCENE I

Saint Alban's.

"*Gloster.* Why, Suffolk, England knows thine insolence.
Q. Margaret. And thy ambition, Gloster.
King Henry. I pr'ythee peace,
Good Queen, and whet not on these furious peers,
For *blessed are the peacemakers on earth.*"

["Blessed are the peacemakers."]—Matt. v. 9.

ACT II. SCENE I.

Enter an inhabitant of St. Alban's, crying "A miracle."

"*Inhabitant.* A miracle ! a miracle !
Suffolk. Come to the king, and tell him what miracle.
Inhabitant. Forsooth, a *blind man* at St. Alban's shrine,
Within this half hour *hath received his sight;*
A man that *ne'er saw in his life before.*
King Henry. Now, God be praised ! that to believing souls
Gives light in darkness, comfort in despair!
(*Enter the Mayor of St. Alban's, attended.*)
Cardinal. Here come the townsmen on procession,
To present your highness with the man.
King Henry. Great is his comfort in this earthly vale,
Although by his sight his sin be multiplied.
Gloster. Stand by, my masters, bring him near the king,
His highness' pleasure is to talk with him.
King Henry. Good fellow, tell us here the circumstance,
That we for thee may glorify the Lord.
What, hast thou been *long blind,* and now restored ?
Simpcox. Born *blind,* an't please your grace.
Simpcox's wife. Ay, indeed, was he.
Suffolk. What woman is this?
Wife. His wife, an't like your worship.
Gloster. Had'st *thou been his mother, thou could'st* have better told.

King Henry. Where wert thou born?
Simpcox. At Berwick in the north, an't like your grace.
King Henry. Poor soul! God's goodness hath been great to thee:
Let never day nor night unhallowed pass,
But still remember what the Lord hath done."

The account here given of this miracle, an imposition recorded in English history, is thus far so scriptural in sentiment, and even diction, that Shakespeare seems as much indebted to Holy Writ as to English history.

"God be praised! that *to believing souls
Gives light in darkness, comfort in despair!*"

The prophet Micah says, too—

"*When I fall, I shall arise; when I sit in darkness, the Lord shall be a light unto me.*" Micah vii. 8.

King Henry says to the man—

"Great is his comfort, *although by his sight his sin be multiplied.*"

Some of the Pharisees said, in the 9th chapter of St. John—

"Are we blind also?"

And they were thus answered—

"If ye were blind, ye should have no sin: *but now ye say, We see; therefore your sin remaineth.*" John ix. 40, 41.

In this chapter of St. John a man *born blind* is *restored to sight*. After this restoration to sight, *the parents* of the person made whole have the following question put to them—

" Is this your son, who ye say *was born blind ?* "

They answer—

" *We know* that this is our son, and *that he was born blind.*"

Now Gloster says to the impostor's wife, when she *seconds* the answer made by him, that he *was born blind*—

" Had'st thou been *his mother,* thou could'st *have better* told."

" *King Henry* (to *Simpcox*).—God's goodness hath been great to thee."

Nahum the prophet says, too—

" *The Lord is good, a stronghold in the day of trouble.*" Nahum i. 7.

Again—

ACT II. SCENE I.

" *King Henry.* O God, what *mischiefs* work the wicked ones ;
Heaping confusion on their own heads thereby!"

The idea in *italics* is thus expressed in the 7th Psalm—

" His *mischief* shall *return upon his own head.*" Psalm vii. 16.

ACT II.   SCENE III.

A Hall of Justice.

[Flourish.] *Enter King* HENRY, *Queen* MARGARET, GLOSTER, *&c. &c., the* DUCHESS, MOTHER JOURDAIN, *&c.*

" *King Henry.* Stand forth, dame Eleanor Cobham, Gloster's wife :
In sight of God and us your guilt is great ;
Receive the sentence of the law, *for sins
Such as by God's book are adjudg'd to death.*"

Gloster's wife is impeached for dealing with witches and with conjurors, in order to destroy King Henry, and certain members of his privy council. Such sins are thus " adjudg'd to death " by Scripture—

" Thou shalt not suffer a witch to live." Exod. xxii. 18.

" A man also or woman that hath a familiar spirit, or that is a wizard, shall surely be put to death : they shall stone them with stones : their blood shall be upon them." Levit. xx. 27.

ACT II.   SCENE III.

London.   A Hall of Justice.

" *King Henry.* Stay, Humphrey Duke of Gloster: ere thou go,
Give up thy staff ; Henry will to himself

Protector be : and God *shall be my hope,*
My stay, my guide, and lantern to my feet."

Here Shakespeare breathes forth, in the person of King Henry, the spirit and devotion of the Psalms—

" Thy word is a *lamp unto my feet, and a light unto my path."*

" Thou art my hiding-place and my shield : I hope in thy word." Psalm cxix. 105, 114.

ACT III. SCENE I

In the speech beginning thus—

" Now, York, or never, steel thy fearful thoughts,"

which York utters in this act, at the end of the first scene, we meet with the following words—

" My brain, *more busy than the labouring spider,*
Weaves tedious snares to trap mine enemies."

[" Weaves tedious snares."]—Such words, at this time, are suitable from the mouth of York. They are undoubtedly taken from Scripture.

The Book of Job contains a passage which shows, in like manner, the instability of the most keen and complex mundane policy—

" The hypocrite's hope shall perish : whose hope shall be cut off, and *whose trust shall be a spider's web."* Job viii. 13, 14.

In the 59th chapter of Isaiah, hypocrites are said

"*To weave the spider's web.*"

"*Their webs*," saith the prophet, "shall not become garments, neither shall they cover themselves with their works: their works," he adds also, "are works of iniquity, and the act of violence is in their hands."

ACT III.   SCENE II.

In Queen Margaret's appeal to Henry VI., Shakespeare may be almost said to quote a passage from the 58th Psalm—

"*Queen.* Be woe for me more wretched than he is.
What, dost thou turn away, and hide thy face?
I am no loathsome leper, look on me.
What, art thou *like the adder waxen deaf?*
Be pois'nous too, and kill thy forlorn queen."

["Adder waxen deaf."]—" They are as venomous *as the poison of a serpent:* even *like the deaf adder.*" Psalm lviii. 4.

Having done with Parts I. and II. of the play of Henry VI., we pass on to the 2nd Act and 5th Scene of the Third Part of it.

The king's soliloquy, which commences with the line—

"This battle fares like to the morning's war,

Contains the sentence—

"To whom God will, there be the victory!"

Sentiments of this kind might be suggested by such a passage recurring to memory as the watchword of Judas " to those about him," in 2 Maccab. xiii. 15 :—

"Victory is of God."

ACT IV.   SCENE I.

The Palace in England.

GLOSTER *and* CLARENCE *present.*
[Flourish]. *Enter* KING EDWARD, LADY GREY, *as Queen*, PEMBROKE, STAFFORD, HASTINGS :—

Edward addresses Clarence touching the marriage of the former. The king, by his union with the Lady Grey, has seriously offended his family, Warwick, and Lewis King of France, to whose sister, the Lady Bona, Edward had been affianced by Warwick.

"*K. Edward.* Suppose they take offence without a cause,
They are but Lewis and Warwick; I am Edward,
Your king and Warwick's, and must have my will.

    Gloster. And you shall have your will, because our
        king:
Yet hasty marriage seldom proveth well.
    K. Edward. Yea, brother Richard, are you offended
        too?
Gloster. Not I:
No, God forbid, that *I should wish them sever'd
Whom God hath join'd together.*"

" What therefore God hath joined together, let not man put asunder." Matthew xix. 6., & Mark x. 9.

ACT V.   SCENE I.

Coventry.

Enter CLARENCE *with Drums and Colours.*

Clarence deserts his father-in-law, and the Red Rose party to which he belongs; and thus addresses Warwick—

    " *Clarence.* Father of Warwick, know you what this
        means?   (*Taking the red rose out of his cap.*)
Look here, I throw my infamy at thee:
I will not ruinate my father's house,
Who gave his blood to lime the stones together,
And set up Lancaster. Why trow'st thou, Warwick,
That Clarence is so harsh, so blunt, unnatural,
To bend the fatal instruments of war
Against his brother and his lawful king?
Perhaps thou wilt object my holy oath:
*To keep that oath, were more impiety
Than Jephthah's, when he sacrificed his daughter.*"

["More impiety than Jephthah's."]—"And Jephthah *vowed a vow unto the Lord*, and said, If thou shalt without fail deliver the children of Ammon into mine hands,

"Then it shall be, that *whatsoever cometh forth of the doors of my house to meet me*, when I r*eturn in peace* from the children of Ammon, shall surely be the Lord's, and *I will offer it up for a burnt-offering.* So Jephthah passed over unto the children of Ammon *to fight against them;* and the Lord *delivered them into his hands.*   *   *   *   *   *

" And Jephthah came to Mizpeh unto his house, and, behold, *his daughter* came out to meet him with timbrels and with dances: and she was his only child; beside her he had neither son nor daughter.

" And it came to pass, when he saw her, that he rent his clothes, and said, Alas, my daughter! thou hast brought me very low, and thou art one of them that trouble me: for I have *opened my mouth unto the Lord, and I cannot go back.*

" And he sent her away for two months: And it came to pass, at the end of two months, that she returned unto her father, *who did with her according to his vow which he had vowed.*"   Judges xi. 30—35, 39.

ACT V. SCENE II,

A Field of Battle near BARNET.

"*Warwick.* Ah, who is nigh? come to me friend or foe,
And tell me who is victor, York or Warwick?
Why ask I that? my mangled body shows,
My blood, my want of strength, my sick heart shows,

That I must yield my body to the earth,
And, by my fall, the conquest to my foe.
*Thus yields the cedar to the axe's edge,
Whose arms gave shelter to the princely eagle,
Under whose shade the ramping lion slept.*"

Steevens seems to consider, not unreasonably, that the 31st chapter of the prophet Ezekiel suggested these images to Shakespeare.

["Thus yields the cedar."]—" Behold the Assyrian *was a cedar* in Lebanon *with fair branches, and with a shadowing shroud, and of an high stature;* and his top was among the thick boughs. * * *

"*All the fowls of heaven made their nests in his boughs,* and *under his branches did all the beasts of the field bring forth their young,* and under his shadow dwelt all great nations.

"Thus was he fair in his greatness, in the length of his branches : for his root was by great waters. * *

"Therefore thus saith the Lord God, Because thou hast lifted up thyself in height, and he hath shot up his top among the thick boughs, and his heart is lifted up in his height; I have therefore delivered him into the hand of the mighty one of the heathen ; he shall surely deal with him : I have driven him out for his wickedness.

"*And strangers,* the terrible of the nations, *have cut him off, and have left him :* upon the mountains and in all the valleys *his branches are fallen,* and his boughs are broken by all the rivers of the land ; and *all the people of the earth are gone down from his shadow, and have left him.*" Ezek. xxxi. 3—7, 10—12.

ACT V. SCENE VII.

"*King Edward IV.* Clarence and Gloster, love my
   lovely queen;
And kiss your princely nephew, brothers both.
   Clarence. The duty that I owe unto your majesty,
I seal upon the lips of this sweet babe.
   King Edward. Thanks, noble Clarence; worthy
   brother, thanks.
   Gloster. And, that I love the tree from whence thou
   sprang'st,
Witness the loving kiss I give the fruit :—
To say the truth, *so Judas kissed his Master ;
And cried, All hail ! when as he meant—all harm.*"
                                                    (Aside.)

The *perfidy of Judas* will be met with in several more instances: we will here introduce an instance from " As You Like It," to show *what a different shade of meaning is there attached* to it to what is here observable.

CHAPTER X.

AS YOU LIKE IT.—*A Comedy.*
ACT III. SCENE IV.

A Cottage in the Forest. Enter ROSALIND *and* CELIA. ROSALIND *in Boy's Clothes for* GANIMED.

"*Rosalind.* Never talk to me, I will weep.
Celia. Do, I pr'ythee; but yet have the grace to consider, that *tears do not become a man.*
Rosalind. But have I not cause to weep?
Celia. As good cause as one would desire; therefore weep.
Rosalind. His *very* hair is of the dissembling colour.
Celia. Something *browner than Judas'*: marry, *his kisses are Judas' own children.*"

["So Judas kissed his Master."]—"And forthwith he (Judas) came to Jesus, and said, *Hail, Master; and kissed him.*" Matt. xxvi. 49.

CHAPTER XI.

THE PLAY OF RICHARD THE SECOND.

ACT I. SCENE I.

The ominous charge made against Mowbray, Duke of Norfolk, by Bolingbroke, in the king's presence, is rendered most effective by the way in which Shakespeare has woven into it a passage of Holy Writ relative to Abel's murder.

"*Bolingbroke.* Further I say—and further will maintain
Upon his bad life, to make all this good—
That he did plot the Duke of Gloster's death;
Suggest his soon-believing adversaries;
And consequently, like a traitor coward,
Sluic'd out his innocent soul through streams of blood:
Which blood, *like sacrificing Abel's, cries*
Even from the tongueless caverns of the earth,
To me, for justice and rough chastisement."

["Which blood, like sacrificing Abel's, cries."]—

"What hast thou done? the voice of thy brother's blood crieth unto me from the grouud.

"And now art thou cursed from the earth, which hath opened her mouth to receive thy brother's blood from thy hand." Gen. iv. 10, 11.

ACT I. SCENE I.

"*King Richard.* Rage must be withstood :
Give me his gage : lions make *leopards tame.*
Norfolk. Yea, *but not change their spots.*"

"*Can the Ethiopian change his skin,* or *the leopard his spots ?*" saith the prophet Jeremiah, from whom Shakespeare took this idea of the leopard, "Then may ye also do good, that are accustomed to do evil." Jer. xiii. 23.

In the 2nd Scene of this Act, there is a striking passage in the Duchess of Gloster's first speech to John o' Gaunt, which may have been furnished by Rev. xvii.

The DUKE OF LANCASTER'S *Palace.*
Enter GAUNT *and the* DUCHESS OF GLOSTER.

"*Gaunt.* Alas! the part I had in Gloster's blood
Doth more solicit me, than your exclaims,
To stir against the butchers of his life.
But, since correction lieth in those hands,
Which made the fault that we cannot correct,
Put we our quarrel to the will of heaven ;
Who when he sees the hours ripe on earth,
Will rain hot vengeance on offenders' heads.

Duchess. Finds brotherhood in thee no sharper spur ?
Hath love in thy old blood no living fire ?
Edward's *seven sons,* whereof thyself art one,
Were as seven phials of his sacred blood."

[" Seven Phials."]—" And there came one of the seven angels *which had the seven vials,* and talked with me, saying unto me, Come hither." Rev. xvii. 1.

Shakespeare in the 3rd Scene, again, seems to have borrowed an expression from the same chapter of Revelation, when Norfolk solemnly attests his innocence to Bolingbroke.

" *Norfolk.* No, Bolingbroke ; if ever I were traitor, *my name be blotted from the book of life.*"

[" Book of life."]—" Whose names were not written in the book of life." Rev. xvii. 8.

ACT III. SCENE II.

Scripture and Shakespeare are somewhat alike, if comparison be made between the sentiments in these two passages—

" *Scroop. Men judge by the complexion of the sky*
   The state and inclination of the day ;
So may you by my dull and heavy eye,
   My tongue hath but a heavier tale to say."
" *Ye can discern the face of the sky ;* but can ye not discern the signs of the times ?" Matt. xvi. 3.

The speech of Richard's unhappy queen, when

she hears "black tidings" relative to the king, indebted for much pathos to Scripture, finely portrays that violent grief which is the prelude to despair.

ACT III. SCENE IV.

Langley.—The Duke of York's Garden.

" *Queen. O I am press'd to death,*
Through want of speaking! "
(*Coming from her concealment.*)

So Job—

"Now, if I hold my tongue, I shall give up the ghost." Job xiii. 19.

" (To Gardener.) *Thou, old Adam's likeness,*
Set to dress this garden, how dares
Thy harsh-rude tongue sound this unpleasing news ?
What Eve, what serpent hath suggested thee
To make a second fall of cursed man ? "

Henry V. says also of Scroop, in Act 2 Scene 2 :—

" I will weep for thee ;
For this revolt of thine, methinks, is like
Another fall of man."

[" Adam's likeness, set to dress this garden."]—" And the Lord God took the man, and *put him into the garden* of Eden *to dress it, and to keep it.*" Gen. ii. 15.

[" What Eve, what serpent hath suggested thee."]—

"And the man said, *The woman*, whom thou gavest to be with me, *she gave me of the tree*, and I did eat.

"And the Lord God *said unto the woman, What is this that thou hast done?* and the woman said, *The serpent beguiled me* and I did eat. * * *

"Because thou hast *hearkened unto the voice of thy wife*, and hast eaten of the tree, of which I commanded thee saying, Thou shalt not eat of it: *cursed is the ground for thy sake;* in sorrow shalt thou eat of it all the days of thy life." Gen. iii. 12, 13, 17.

ACT IV. SCENE I.

BOLINGBROKE *to* BISHOP *of* CARLISLE.

"*Bolingbroke.* Why, bishop, is Norfolk dead?
Carlisle. As sure as I live, my lord.
Bolingbroke. Sweet peace *conduct his sweet soul to the bosom*
Of good Old Abraham!"*

["Bosom of good old Abraham."]—"And it came to pass that the beggar died, *and was carried by angels into Abraham's bosom.*" Luke xvi. 22.

It is singular that Shakespeare should have put these words, which are applied to Lazarus in the parable of Dives and Lazarus, into Bolingbroke's

---

* FROM RICHARD III.

"*Richard III.* The sons of Edward sleep in *Abraham's bosom.*" Here the words "*Abraham's bosom*" are used (as in the parable and the case above) to denote *release* from an abject state of existence.

mouth; they were, however, as applicable to Norfolk as to Lazarus, if a good man; for he had been banished by the king for life, and was consequently *stripped* of all his possessions.

ACT IV.   SCENE I.

These words of Bolingbroke,

" In God's name I'll ascend the regal throne,"

elicit from the Bishop of Carlisle the following able and indignant speech :—

" *Carlisle*. Marry, God forbid !
Worst in this royal presence may I speak,
Yet best beseeming me to speak the truth.
Would God, that any in this noble presence
Were enough noble to be upright judge
Of noble Richard; then true nobless would
Learn him forbearance from so foul a wrong.
What subject can give sentence on his king ?
And who sits here, that is not Richard's subject?
Thieves are not judg'd, but they are by to hear,
Although apparent guilt be seen in them :
* And shall *the* FIGURE *of God's majesty*,
His captain, steward, deputy elect,
Anointed, crowned, planted many years,
Be judg'd by subject and inferior breath,
And he himself not present ? O forbid it, God,

---

* In the *image* of God made he man." Gen. ix. 6.

That in a Christian clime, souls refin'd
Should show so heinous, black, obscene a deed!
I speak to subjects, and a subject speaks,
Stirr'd up by Heaven thus boldly for his king.
My lord of Hereford here, whom you call king,
Is a foul traitor to proud Hereford's king:
And if you crown him, let me prophesy—
The blood of English shall manure the ground,
And future ages groan for this foul act;
Peace shall go sleep with Turks and Infidels,
And, in this seat of peace, tumultuous wars
Shall kin with kin, and kind with kind confound;
Disorder, horror, fear, and mutiny,
Shall here inhabit, and this land be call'd
The field *of Golgotha, and dead men's skulls.*"

["Golgotha, and dead men's skulls."]—" And when they were come unto a place called *Golgotha, that is to say, a place of a skull."* Matt. xxvii. 33.

And Mark thus—

"And they bring him unto *the place Golgotha,* which is, being interpreted, *the place of a skull.*" Mark xv. 22.

In Job xxxiv. 18, it is said—

"Is it fit to say to a king, Thou art wicked? and to princes, Ye are ungodly?"

"Oh! if you rear this house against this house,
It will the woefullest division prove"—

"If a house be divided against itself, that house cannot stand." Mark iii. 25—

"That ever fell upon this cursed earth :
Prevent, resist it, let it not be so,
Lest child, child's children, cry against you—woe!"

Thus does the dignified prelate, regardless of his own safety, address the proud usurper of Richard's throne, with all the simplicity, yet blighting energy, of eloquence demanding justice, and execrating oppression.

ACT IV. SCENE I.

London. Westminster Hall.

The passages about to follow, are uttered by Richard the Second when he is deprived of his power, and they attest, like the words of his queen, this melancholy truth—that lofty minds, when harassed by the prospect of annihilation, protracted by torture, are wont to vent their agony in Scripture language; sentences being passionately spoken which almost startle us by their abrupt reference to the obliquity and depravity of human nature.

Re-enter YORK *with* KING RICHARD, *and Officers bearing the Crown.*

"*King Richard.* Alack! why am I sent for to a king,
Before I have shook off the regal thoughts
Wherewith I reign'd? I hardly yet have learn'd
To insinuate, flatter, bow, and bend my knee :
Give sorrow leave awhile to tutor me
To this submission. Yet I well remember
The favours of these men : Were they not mine?

Did they not sometime cry, *All hail! to me?*
So Judas did to Christ: but he, in twelve,
Found truth in all, but one; I, in twelve thousand,
none."

ACT III. SCENE II.

When the king asks for tidings relative to Wiltshire, Bagot, Bushy, Green, and in his agitation imagines that they have deserted him and made peace with Bolingbroke; and Scroop returns this vague answer,

"*Scroop.* Peace have they made with him, indeed, my lord,"

the king, amongst other stern invectives of fiery wrath, thunders forth this notable and bitter sentence—

" *Three Judases,* each one *thrice worse than Judas!* "

["*Judas.*"]—" And while he yet spake, *lo, Judas, one of the twelve,* came, and with him a great multitude with swords and staves, from the chief priests and elders of the people.

"Now he that betrayed him gave them a sign, saying, Whomsoever I shall kiss, that same is he: hold him fast.

"And forthwith he came to Jesus, and said, Hail Master, and kissed him." Matt. xxvi. 47, 48, 49.

["He, in twelve, found truth in all, but one."]—

"Now, when the even was come, he sat down with the twelve.

"And as they did eat, he said, Verily I say unto you, that *one* of you shall betray me." Matt. xxvi. 20, 21.

Again,

ACT IV.   SCENE I.

"*King Richard.* What more remains?
Northumberland. No more, but that you read
(*Offering a paper*)
These accusations, and these grievous crimes,
Committed by your person and your followers,
Against the state and profit of this land;
That, by confessing them, the souls of men
May deem that you are worthily depos'd.
  King Richard. Must I do so? and must I ravel out
My weav'd up follies? Gentle Northumberland,
If thy offences were upon record,
Would it not shame thee in so fair a troop,
To read a lecture of them? If thou would'st,
There should'st thou find *one heinous article*,
Containing the deposing of a king,
And cracking the strong warrant of an oath,
Mark'd with a blot, damn'd in the book of heaven."

["Cracking the strong warrant of an oath."]—"As I live, saith the Lord God, surely in the place where the king dwelleth that made *him* king, *whose oath he despised, and whose covenant he brake, even with him in the midst of Babylon he shall die.*

"Neither shall Pharaoh, with his mighty army and

great company, make for him in the war, by casting up mounts, and building forts, to cut off many persons.

"*Seeing he despised the oath by breaking the covenant, when lo, he had given his hand,* and hath done all these things, he *shall not escape.*

"Therefore thus saith the Lord God, As I live, surely *mine oath that he hath despised,* and *my covenant that he hath broken,* even it *will I recompense upon his own head.*" Ezek. xvii. 16, 17, 18, 19.

"*King Richard.* Nay, all of you, that stand and look
upon me,
Whilst that my wickedness doth bait myself,
Though some of you, *with. Pilate, wash your hands,*
Showing an outward pity ; yet you Pilates
Have here deliver'd me to my sour cross,
And water cannot wash away your sin."

["With Pilate wash your hands."]—"When Pilate saw that he could prevail nothing, but that rather a tumult was made, *he took water, and washed his hands* before the multitude, saying, I am innocent of the blood of this just person : see ye to it.

"Then answered all the people, and said, His blood be on us, and on our children.

"Then released he Barabbas unto them : and when he had scourged Jesus, he delivered him to be crucified." Matt. xxvii. 24—26.

Though some of you, says the king, seem to feel compassion for me, and would fain be rid of the odium attached to these proceedings; you are notwithstanding, like Pilate, who washed his hands before the multitude, but delivered up our Lord to be scourged and crucified.

ACT V. SCENE V.

Pomfret.
The Dungeon of the Castle.

"*King Richard.* I have been studying how to compare
This prison where I live, unto the world:
And, for because the world is populous,
And here is not a creature but myself,
I cannot do it;—Yet I'll hammer it out.
My *brain* I'll prove the *female* to my *soul;*
My *soul*, the *father:* and these two beget
A generation of still breeding thoughts,
And these same thoughts people this little world;
In humours like the people of this world,
For no thought is contented. The better sort—
As thoughts of things divine—are intermix'd
With scruples, and do set the *word itself*
Against the word:
As thus—*Come little ones;* and then again—
It is as hard to come, as for a camel
To thread the postern of a needle's eye."

Shakespeare is indebted no little to Holy Writ for a soliloquy pregnant with philosophy of so peculiar yet devout a cast.

The passage—

"It is as hard to come, as for a camel
To thread the postern of a needle's eye,"

may be derived either from Matt. xix. 24,

"And again I say unto you, It is easier for a camel to go through the eye of a needle, than for a rich man to enter into the *kingdom of God.*"

Or from Mark x. 24, 25—

"But Jesus answereth again, and saith unto them, *Children,* how hard is it for them that trust in riches *to enter into the kingdom* of God!

"It is easier, &c."

The same may be said of *Come, little ones.* It may either be derived from Matt. xix. 13, 14—

"Then were there brought unto him *little children,* that he should put his hands on them, and pray : and the disciples rebuked them. But Jesus said, *Suffer little children,* and forbid them not, to *come unto* me; for of SUCH is the *kingdom of heaven.*"

Or Mark x. 13, 14—

"And they brought young children to him, that he should touch them : and his disciples rebuked those that brought them. But when Jesus saw it, he was much displeased, and said unto them, Suffer *the little children* to *come unto me,* and forbid them not; for of SUCH is the *kingdom of God.*"

The idea—

"My brain I'll prove the female to my soul; my soul the father," might be suggested to the poet's fertile mind by what is said of *marriage* in either of the chapters mentioned, *conjoined with the recent remark* which fell from the king's lips when about to bid a final adieu to his queen:—

"*Richard.* Doubly divorced—bad men, ye violate
A twofold marriage; 'twixt my *crown* and *me;*
And then betwixt me and my married wife."

Thus, Matt. xix. 3, 4, 5—

"The Pharisees also came unto him, tempting him, and saying unto him, Is it lawful for a man to put away his wife for every cause? And he answered and said unto them, Have ye not read, that he which made them at the beginning, made them *male* and *female*, and said, For this cause shall a man leave father and mother, and shall cleave to his wife; and they twain shall be one flesh?"

Or Mark x. 2 to 8—

"And the Pharisees came to him, and asked him, Is it lawful for a man to put away his wife? tempting him.

"And he answered and said unto them, What did Moses command you?

"And they said, Moses suffered to write a bill of divorcement, and to put her away.

"And Jesus answered and said unto them, For the hardness of your heart he wrote you this precept.

"But from the beginning of the creation God made them *male* and *female*.

"For this cause shall a man leave his father and mother, and cleave to his wife;
"And the twain shall be one flesh: so then they are no more twain, but one flesh."

ACT V. SCENE VI.

The following passage occurs in the speech delivered to Exton, Richard's murderer, by Bolingbroke, now King Henry IV.:—

"*Bolingbroke.* The guilt of conscience take thou for
    thy labour,
But neither my good word nor princely favour:
With Cain, go wander through the shade of night,
And never show thy head by day nor light."

["With Cain go wander."]—Words of similar import are observable in the judgment pronounced upon Cain after the murder of Abel:—

"When thou tillest the ground, it shall not henceforth yield unto thee her strength; *a fugitive and a vagabond shalt thou be in the earth.*" Gen. iv. 12.

The expressions of Richard, shortly before and after his resignation, incontestably prove how well Shakespeare knew the effects of mental torture, and how truly he could fathom the depths of despair. In the play of Henry IV., Sir John Falstaff is as facetiously true to nature as Richard II. is mournfully so. Falstaff is a wag, a liar, and an epicure; but he interests us with his wit, his artifice, and his impudence; for we hear undisturbed his racy jokes when he amuses the prince and his associates with mock pathos and bombast sentiments. Falstaff is one of the loose persons which the profligate Prince of Wales entertains to aid and abet him in all his mad pranks and wanton follies. Having thus introduced Falstaff, we proceed to the last point to be considered before we investigate the play; viz., *why* we find *the words of wisdom* in his mouth. Falstaff is the *reverse* of Richard: what then? extremes naturally produce similar results: Shakespeare *knew* it, and has in this respect drawn the characters truthfully. That which causes Richard to quote Scripture is abject misery: that which causes Falstaff to do it is thoughtless levity. Falstaff is dead to all religion; he acts up to the false and, as it proves to him, *ruinous* maxim, "Let us eat and drink, for to-morrow we die." He "glories in his shame," revelling in jokes relating to it, in the very words of Scripture; for he delights to stray upon holy ground, and seems never more animated than when indulging in such impiety himself, and encouraging it in the prince, his master.

CHAPTER XII.

THE PLAY OF HENRY IV.
ACT I.   SCENE II.
London.   Another Room in the Palace.

"*Falstaff.* . . . . But, Hal, I pr'ythee, trouble me no more with vanity. I would to God thou and I knew where a commodity of good names were to be bought: An old lord of the council rated me the other day in the street about you, sir; but I marked him not: and yet *he talked very wisely; but I regarded him not:* and yet *he talked wisely, and in the street, too.*

Prince Henry. Thou did'st well; for *wisdom cries out in the streets, and no man regards it.*"

["Wisdom cries out in the streets, and no man regards it."]—"*Wisdom crieth without; she uttereth her voice in the streets:* she crieth in the chief place of concourse, in the openings of the gates: in the city she uttereth her words, saying—

"How long, ye simple ones, will ye love simplicity?

And the scorners delight in their scorning, and fools hate knowledge?

"Turn you at my reproof: behold, I will pour out my spirit unto you—I will make known my words unto you.

"*Because I have called*, and ye refused; I have stretched out my hand, *and no man regarded:* but ye have *set at naught all my counsel,* and would *none of my reproof:* I also will laugh at your calamity; I will mock when your fear cometh: When your fear cometh as desolation, and your destruction cometh as a whirlwind; when distress and anguish cometh upon you." Prov. i. 20—27.

The above example from Henry IV. is part of the first dialogue between Falstaff and Prince Henry: they playfully refer in it to the disgraceful pastimes and outrages which they are in the habit of perpetrating by night, and make the ruin to which such conduct leads men, matter for wit and repartee.

ACT II.   SCENE IV.

Eastcheap. A Room in the Boar's Head Tavern.

Falstaff again notes Scripture when, personating the King, he describes himself (Falstaff) as a suitable companion for the young prince.

* * * * * * * *

"*Falstaff.* There is a thing, Harry, which thou hast

often heard of, and is known to many in our land by
the name of *pitch: this pitch*, as ancient writers do
report, *doth defile; so doth the company thou keepest:*
for, Harry, now I do not speak to thee in drink, but
in tears; not in pleasure, but in passion; not in words
only, but in woes also: And yet there is a virtuous
man whom I have often noted in thy company, but I
know not his name."

Ecclus. xiii. 1, is in part quoted in the third act
and third scene of Much ado about Nothing:—

" 2nd *Watch.* If we know him to be a thief, shall we
not lay hands on him?
Dogberry. Truly, by your office you may; but, I
think, *they that touch pitch will be defil'd."*

In Second Part of Henry VI., act ii. scene i., we
also find this example:—

" *Glos.* Noble she is; but, if she have forgot
Honour, and virtue, and convers'd with such
As, *like to pitch, defile nobility."*

["Pitch doth defile."]—"He *that toucheth pitch* shall
be *defiled therewith;* and he that hath fellowship *with
a proud man*, shall be like unto him." Ecclus. xiii. 1.

" *Prince Henry.* What manner of man, an it like
your Majesty?
Falstaff. A good portly man, i' faith, and a corpulent;
of a cheerful look, a pleasing eye, and a most noble carriage; and, as I think, his age some fifty, or, by'r lady,
inclining to threescore; and, now I remember me, his

name is Falstaff: If that man should be lewdly given, he deceiveth me; for, Harry, I see virtue in his looks. *If then, the tree may be known by the fruit, as the fruit by the tree,* then, peremptorily I speak it, there is virtue in that Falstaff: him keep with, the rest banish."

["As the tree by the fruit."]—"Either make the tree good and his fruit good; or else make the tree corrupt and his fruit corrupt: for the tree is known by his fruit." Matt. xii. 33.

After this Prince Henry says to Falstaff—

"Dost thou speak like a king? Do thou stand for me, and I'll play my father.

Falstaff. Depose me? if *thou* dost it [*i.e.*, act the part of your father] half so gravely, so majestically both in word and matter, hang me up by the heels for a rabbet-sucker, or a poulter's hare.

Prince Henry. Well, here I am set.

Falstaff. And here I stand:—judge, my masters.

Prince Henry. Now, Harry, whence come you?

Falstaff. My noble lord, from Eastcheap.

Prince Henry. The complaints I hear of thee are grievous.

Falstaff. 'Sblood, my lord, they are false! . . .

Prince Henry. Swearest thou, ungracious boy? henceforth ne'er look on me. Thou art violently carried away from grace: there is a devil haunts thee in the likeness of a fat old man; a tun of man is thy companion. Why dost thou converse with * * * * * * * that roasted Manningtree ox, that grey iniquity, that father ruffian, that vanity in years? Wherein is he good, but to taste sack and drink it? wherein neat and cleanly, but to carve a capon and eat it? wherein cunning, but in craft? wherein crafty, but in villainy? wherein villainous, but in all things? wherein worthy, but in nothing?

Falstaff. I would your grace would take me with you;

Whom means your grace?

Prince Henry. That villainous, abominable misleader of youth,

Falstaff, that old white-bearded Satan.

Falstaff. My lord, the man I know.

Prince Henry. I know thou dost.

Falstaff. But to say I know more harm in him than in myself, were to say more than I know. That he is old (the more the pity), his white hairs do witness it: *   *   *   *   *   *

If to be old and merry be a sin, then many an old host that I know is damn'd: *if to be fat be to be hated, then Pharaoh's lean kine are to be loved.* No, my good lord; banish Peto, banish Bardolph, banish Poins: but for sweet Jack Falstaff, kind Jack Falstaff, true Jack Falstaff, valiant Jack Falstaff, and therefore more valiant, being, as he is, old Jack Falstaff, banish not him thy Harry's company—banish not him thy Harry's company; banish plump Jack, and banish all the world.

Prince Henry. I do, I will."

["Pharaoh's lean kine are to be loved."]—This thought may be supposed to spring from the comparison made when the Prince, speaking of Falstaff, says *that roasted Manningtree ox.* "If," says Falstaff, "to be *fat* be to be *hated*, then *Pharaoh's lean kine,* which *devoured* the *fat* kine, *are to be loved.*" The retort seems to be to this effect: "*The wicked devoureth the man* that is *more righteous* than he." Habak. i. 13.

["Pharaoh's lean kine."]—"And Pharaoh said unto Joseph, In my dream, behold, I stood upon the bank of the river: and, behold, there came up out of the river seven kine, fat-fleshed and well-favoured; and they fed in a meadow:

"And, behold, seven other kine came up after them, poor and very ill-favoured, and lean-fleshed, such as I never saw in all the land of Egypt for badness: and the lean and the ill-favoured kine did *eat up* the first seven fat kine: and when they *had eaten them up*, it *could not be known* that they *had eaten them*; but they were still ill-favoured, as at the beginning." Gen. xli. 17—21.

ACT III. SCENE II

In the speech which opens thus, "God pardon thee," are the words—

"They surfeited with honey; and began
To loathe the taste of sweetness."

So Proverbs—

"*The full soul loatheth an honeycomb;* but to the hungry soul every bitter thing is sweet." Proverbs xxvii. 7.

The King here cautions the Prince of Wales against the habit of making himself—

" So stale and cheap to vulgar company."

An error which the late king committed, and thereby lost the respect of his subjects.

ACT III. SCENE III.

Eastcheap. A Room in the Boar's Head Tavern.
FALSTAFF *to* BARDOLPH.

"*Falstaff.* Do thou amend thy face, and I'll amend my life: Thou art our admiral, thou bearest the lantern in the poop—but 'tis in *the nose of thee;* thou art *the knight of the burning lamp.*

Bardolph. Why, Sir John, my face does you no harm.

Falstaff. No, I'll be sworn; I make as good use of it as many a man doth of *a death's head,* or *a memento mori:* I never see thy face but *I think upon hell-fire, and Dives that lived in purple; for there he is in his robes, burning, burning.*"

["And Dives that lived in purple."]—There was a certain rich man, *which was clothed in purple and fine linen,* and fared sumptuously every day:

" And *there was a certain beggar named Lazarus, which was laid at his gate, full of sores,*

" And desiring to be fed with the crumbs which fell from the rich man's table: *moreover, the dogs came and licked his sores.*

" And it came to pass that the beggar died, and was

carried by the angels into Abraham's bosom : the rich man also died, and was buried ;

"*And in hell he lifted up his eyes, being in torments*, and seeth Abraham afar off, and Lazarus in his bosom.

"And he cried, and said, Father Abraham, have mercy on me, and send Lazarus, that he may dip the tip of his finger in water, and cool my tongue ; *for I am tormented in this flame.*" Luke xvi. 19—24.

Falstaff says to Bardolph, who, by the way, brings these remarks upon himself, "I make as good use of *it* [*thy face*, which reminds me of thy vices] as many a man doth of *a death's head*, or a *memento mori :* I never see thy face but I *think upon* hell-fire," &c.

A death's head, or a *memento mori*, makes, doubtless, many a man *think upon* hell-fire; but if men derive no solid benefit, if they *amend not their lives*, what doth it profit them? Falstaff renders himself, as many profligate wits do, amenable to this censure, " As a thorn goeth up into the hand of a drunkard, so is a parable in the mouth of fools." Prov. xxvi. 9.

ACT III. SCENE III.

Reference is now made, by the hostess of the Boar's Head Tavern, to a conversation that has passed between Falstaff and herself respecting the knight's ring.

The subject of the ring was started by the knight in the following manner :—

"Shall I not take mine ease iu mine inn, but I shall have my pocket pick'd? I have lost a seal-ring of my grandfather's, worth forty marks.
Hostess. Nay, my lord [to Prince Henry,] he called
   you Jack, and said he would cudgel you.
Falstaff. Did I, Bardolph?
Bardolph. Indeed, Sir John, you said so.
Falstaff. Yea; if he said my ring was copper.
P. Henry. I say, 'tis copper: Dar'st thou be as good
   as thy word now?
Falstaff. Why, Hal, thou know'st, as thou art but
   man, I dare: but, as thou art prince, I fear
   thee, *as I fear the roaring of the lion's whelp.*
P. Henry. And why not, as the lion?
Falstaff. The king himself is to be feared as the lion."

The ideas, *as I fear the roaring of the lion's whelp,* and *why not as the lion? the king himself is to be feared as the lion,* evidently take their origin from the second verse of the twentieth chapter of Proverbs—"The fear of a king is as the roaring of a lion." We can best defend this statement by supplying the ellipsis to the words—and *why not as the lion?* and *why not* (i.e.) *fear me as the roaring of the lion?*

Again,

ACT III. SCENE III.

"*Falstaff.* Dost thou hear, Hal? Thou knowest, *in the state of innocency, Adam fell;* and what should poor Jack Falstaff do, in the days of villainy? Thou seest I have more flesh than another man; and therefore more frailty."

["State of innocency, Adam fell."]—It is surely allowable in this case to refer the reader to the play of Richard II. Falstaff's wit needs no comment.

PART I. ACT IV. SCENE II.

"*Falstaff.* I pressed me none but such toasts and butter, with hearts in their bellies no bigger than pins' heads, and they have bought out their services; and now my whole charge consists of ancients, corporals, lieutenants, gentlemen of companies, slaves *as ragged as Lazarus in the painted cloth, where the glutton's dogs licked his sores;* and such as, indeed, were never soldiers; but discarded unjust serving-men, younger sons to younger brothers, revolted tapsters, and ostlers tradefallen; the cankers of a calm world, and a long peace; ten times more dishonourably ragged than an old-faced ancient; and such have I to fill up the rooms of them that have bought out their services, that you would think that *I had a hundred and fifty tattered prodigals, lately come from swine-keeping, from eating draff and husks.*"

["Prodigals, lately come from swine-keeping."]—" A certain man had two sons: and *the younger of them said to his father, Father, give me the portion of goods that falleth to me. And he divided unto them his living. And not many days after, the younger son gathered all together, and took his journey into a far country, and there wasted his substance with riotous living. And when he had spent all, there arose a mighty famine in that land; and he began to be in want. And he went and joined himself to a citizen of that country; and he sent him into his fields to feed swine. And he would fain have filled his belly with the husks that the swine did eat; and no man gave unto him.*" Luke xv. 11—15.

The graphic descriptions given, by Shakespeare's allusions to the parables of Dives and Lazarus, and the prodigal son, have the intended effect upon us; they render the mean appearance of these wretches as despicable as poverty can make it, because it is said to spring from a course of deliberate iniquity. Such creatures were, in one sense, suitable soldiers for Falstaff; they were not likely to blush for their leader's professional defects.

The parable of the prodigal son is mentioned in the Two Gentlemen of Verona.

ACT II.   SCENE III

A Street.   Launce, a clownish servant.

" *Launce.* Nay, 'twill be this hour ere I have done weeping; all the kind of the Launces have this very fault: *I have received my proportion, like the prodigious son*, and am going with Sir Protheus to the imperial's court."

The parable of the prodigal son is alluded to again in As You Like It; severe reproof is, however, given by it in this instance; petty tyranny could hardly be put in a more contemptible light. Thus,

ACT I. SCENE I.

OLIVER *and* ORLANDO, *sons of* SIR ROWLAND DE BOIS.

" *Oliver.* Now, sir! what make you here?
Orlando. Nothing: I am not taught to make any thing.
Oliver. What mar you then, sir?
Orlando. Marry, sir, I am helping you to mar that which God made, a poor unworthy brother of yours, with idleness.
Oliver. Marry, sir, be better employed, and be naught awhile.
Orlando. Shall I keep your hogs, and eat husks with them?
What prodigal portion have I spent, that I should come to such penury?"

We now turn our attention to the Second Part of the play of Henry IV.

ACT I. SCENE I.

In Travers's answer to the Earl of Northumberland's question—

"Now, Travers, what good tidings come with you?"

is this passage—

"With that, he gave his able horse the head,
And, bending forwards, struck his armed heels
Against the panting sides of his poor jade
Up to the rowel-head; and starting so,
He-seem'd in running to devour the way."

["He seemed in running."]—It is said of the war-horse, in 39th chapter of the book of Job—

"*He swalloweth the ground in fierceness and rage.*"
Steevens.

ACT I. SCENE I.

The words of Northumberland, introduced below, reveal his agony of heart when he hears that his rebel army is cowed; and that his son Henry Percy, is slain by the Prince of Wales. Thoroughly roused from his apathy, both by grief and desperation, he now resolves to hazard what remains—to welcome ruin.

"*Northumberland.* For this I shall have time enough
  to mourn.
In poison there is physic; and these news,
Having been well, that would have made me sick,
Being sick, have in some measure made me well:
And as the wretch whose fever-weaken'd joints,
Like strengthless hinges, buckle under life,
Impatient of his fit, breaks like a fire
Out of his keeper's arms; even so my limbs,
Weaken'd with grief, being now enrag'd with grief,
Are thrice themselves: hence, therefore, thou nice
  crutch;
A scaly gauntlet now, with joints of steel,
Must glove this hand; and hence, thou sickly quoif,
Thou art a guard too wanton for the head
Which princes, flesh'd with conquest, aim to hit.
Now bind my brows with iron; and approach
The rugged'st hour that time and spite dare bring,
To frown upon the enrag'd Northumberland!
Let heaven kiss earth! Now let not nature's hand
Keep the wild flood confin'd! let order die!
And let this world no longer be a stage,
To feed contention in *a lingering* act;
But let one spirit of the first-born Cain
Reign in all bosoms."

Mark the vent that this fell swoop of morbid vengeance must needs seek out, or lose the form of utterance—" But let one spirit of the first-born Cain reign in all bosoms." That is, May wrath as fierce as Cain's when he slew his brother, prevail amongst mankind, and cause such sudden and universal carnage, that there be no man to bury the slain! With what tremendous effect does Shakespeare introduce Cain's wrath, and its consequences: "Let the spirit of the first-born Cain reign in all bosoms!" The whole force of the speech seems centred in these few words—

["Spirit of the first-born Cain."]—"The Lord had respect unto Abel and his offering: but unto Cain and his offering he had not respect.

"And Cain was very wroth, and his countenance fell.

"And Cain talked with Abel his brother: and it came to pass, when they were in the field, *that Cain rose up against Abel his brother, and slew him.*" Gen. iv. 4, 5, 6, 8.

ACT I. SCENE II.

London. A Street.
Enter SIR JOHN FALSTAFF, *with his Page bearing his Sword and Buckler.*

"*Falstaff.* What said Master Dombledon about the satin for my short cloak and slops?

Page. He said, sir, you should procure him better assurance than Bardolph: he would not take his bond and yours; he liked not the security.

Falstaff. Let him be damn'd like the glutton! may his tongue be hotter! a whoreson *Achitophel!*"

["Tongue be hotter."]—An allusion to the request made by Dives to the patriarch—

"And he cried, and said, Father Abraham, have mercy on me, and send Lazarus, that *he may dip the*

H

tip of his finger in water, and cool my tongue; for I am tormented in this flame." Luke xvi. 24.

The character of a scoffer, libertine, and brilliant wit, in this short dialogue, is thrown out by the poet in bold relief; yet the bounds of nature are by no means overstepped. Falstaff, by his use of "*Achitophel,*" states, in a characteristic way, that the tailor is more politic than honest. But this is not all. The very *word* "*Achitophel*" is armed with a sting; for it signifies "*Brother of ruin.*"

[Achitophel or Ahithophel.]—" And one told David, saying, Ahithophel is among the conspirators with Absalom. And David said, O Lord, I pray thee turn the counsel of Ahithophel into foolishness." 2 Sam. xv. 31.

" And Absalom and all the men of Israel said, The counsel of Hushai the Archite is better than the counsel of Ahithophel: for the Lord had appointed to defeat the good counsel of Ahithophel, to the intent that the Lord might bring evil upon Absalom." 2 Sam. xvii. 14.

"And when Ahithophel saw that his counsel was not followed, he saddled his ass, and arose, and gat him home to his house, to his city, and put his household in order, and hanged himself, and died, and was buried in the sepulchre of his father." 2 Sam. xvii. 23.

Men too often derive wit from Scripture; men who are good as well as brilliant are thus prone to fall into error. Falstaff, however, is not a good man, and we see the result; his wit is, in several instances, utterly indefensible.

ACT I. SCENE III.

SHAKESPEARE *and* **SCRIPTURE** *compared.*

"*Bardolph.* When we mean to build,
We first survey the plot, then draw the model;
And when we see the figure of the house,
Then must we rate the cost of the erection"

"For which of you, intending to build a tower, sitteth not down first, and counteth the cost, whether he have sufficient to finish it?" Luke xiv. 28.

ACT I. SCENE III.

SHAKESPEARE *and* **SCRIPTURE** *again compared.*

"*Archbishop of York.* Let us on;
And publish the occasion of our arms.
The commonwealth is sick of their own choice,
Their over-greedy love hath surfeited:
A habitation giddy and unsure
Hath he, that buildeth on the vulgar heart.
O thou fond many! with what loud applause
Did'st thou beat Heaven with blessing Bolingbroke,
Before he was what thou would'st have him be?
And being now trimm'd in thine own desires,
Thou, beastly feeder, art so full of him,
That thou *provok'st thyself to cast him up.*
So, so, thou common dog, didst thou disgorge
Thy glutton bosom of the royal Richard;

And now thou wouldst eat thy dead vomit up,
And howl'st to find it."

["Eat thy dead vomit up."]—The above metaphorical idea probably owes its origin to this passage of Scripture :—

"But it happeneth unto them according to the true proverb, The dog is turned to his own vomit again." 2 Peter ii. 22.

In the 3rd Act, 7th scene of Henry V., the passage, 2 Peter ii. 22, is introduced in the following way—

"*Dauphin.* I tell thee, constable, my mistress wears her own hair.
Constable. I could make as true a boast as that, if I had a sow to my mistress.
Dauphin. Le chien est retourné à son propre vomissement, et la truie lavée au bourbier."

ACT II. SCENE II.

"*Poins* [reads]. John Falstaff, knight. Every man must know *that*, as oft as he has occasion to name himself. Even like those that are kin to the king; for they never prick their finger, but they say, *There is some of the king's blood spilt!* How comes that? says he that takes upon him not to conceive: the answer is as ready as a borrower's cap—*I am the king's poor cousin, sir.*

Prince Henry. Nay, they will be *kin to us*, or they will fetch it from *Japhet.*"

["Nay, they will be kin to us."]—No matter, says the prince, how distant their relationship to us is, they will contrive to speak of it whenever they can find occasion for so doing.

["Japhet."]—" Now these are the generations of the sons of Noah, Shem, Ham, and *Japheth :* and unto them were sons born after the flood.

"The sons of *Japheth;* Gomer, and Magog, and Madai, and Javan, and Tubal, and Meschech, and Tiras.

" And the sons of Gomer ; Ashkenaz, and Riphath, and Togarmah.

" And the sons of Javan ; Elishah, and Tarshish, Kittim, and Dodanim.

" By *these were the isles of the Gentiles* divided in their lands ; every one after his tongue, after their families, in their nations." Gen. x. 1—5.

ACT III. SCENE II.

Court before JUSTICE SHALLOW'S *House in Gloucestershire.*

"*Justice Shallow.* O the mad days that I have spent ! and to see how many of my old companions are dead !

Justice Silence. We shall all follow, cousin.

Justice Shallow. Certain, 'tis certain ; very sure, very sure : *death, as the Psalmist saith,* is certain to all ; all shall die."

[" As the Psalmist saith."]—"The days of our age are threescore years and ten ; and though men be so strong that come to fourscore years : yet is their strength then but labour and sorrow; so soon passeth it away, and we are gone." Psalm xc. 10.

As the Merry Wives of Windsor is said to have been written for the purpose of bringing the character of Falstaff again before the public, we have placed this play next to Henry IV., where the character is drawn with masterly effect.

ACT I. SCENE III.

A Room in the Garter Inn.—*Enter* FALSTAFF, HOST, BARDOLPH, NYM, PISTOL, *and* ROBIN.

Falstaff, in the course of conversation, artfully contrives to make Ford's wife the subject of it—

"*Falstaff.* Now, the report goes, she has all the rule of her husband's purse; she hath *legions of angels.*
Pistol. As many *devils* entertain; and, To her, boy, say I."

"They have in England," says Shakespeare, in "The Merchant of Venice"—

"*A coin* that *bears the figure of an angel Stamped in gold;*"—

an angel, when current, was worth *ten shillings.*

Pistol's reply, *as many devils entertain,* makes the play upon the words *legions of angels* most obvious.

["Legions of angels."]—"Thinkest thou that I cannot now pray to my Father, and he shall presently give me more than twelve *legions of angels?*" Matt. xxvi. 53.

ACT II. SCENE I.
Enter FORD, PISTOL, PAGE, *and* NYM.

"*Ford.* Well, I hope it be not so.

Pistol. Hope is a curtail dog in some affairs: Sir John affects thy wife.

Ford. Why, sir, my wife is not young.

Pistol. He woos both high and low, both rich and poor, both young and old, *one with another.*"

The words in *italics* seem to have been by memory transferred from Psalm xlix.; in this Psalm there is a similar mode of expression—

"High and low, rich and poor, one with another." Psalm xlix. 2.

ACT IV. SCENE V.
A Room in the Garter Inn.—Enter HOST *and* SIMPLE.

"*Host.* What wouldst thou have, boor? what, thickskin? speak, breathe, discuss; brief, short, quick, snap.

Simple. Marry, sir, I come to speak with Sir John Falstaff, from Master Slender.

Host. There's his chamber, his house, his castle, his standing-bed, and truckle-bed; 'tis *painted about with the story of the prodigal, fresh and new.*"

["Story of the prodigal."]—"Not many days after, the younger son gathered all together, and took his journey into a far country, and there wasted his substance with riotous living.

"And when he had spent all, there arose a mighty famine in that land; and he began to be in want.

"And he went and joined himself to a citizen of that country; and he sent him into his fields to feed swine.

"And he would fain have filled his belly with the husks that the swine did eat: and no man gave unto him. And when he came to himself, he said, How many hired servants of my father's have bread enough, and to spare, and I perish with hunger! I will arise, and go to my father, and will say unto him, Father, I have sinned against heaven, and before thee, and am no more worthy to be called thy son: make me as one of thy hired servants.

"And he arose, and came to his father. But when he was yet a great way off, his father saw him, and had compassion, and ran, and fell on his neck and kissed him." Luke xv. 13 to end of 20.

["Painted about with the story of the prodigal."] —The story may be supposed to be delineated from the departure of the young man, including his excesses and want, to the period of his return, in abject misery, to implore a father's forgiveness.

Falstaff is addicted to riotous living, and is by no means ignorant of Scripture: the story of the prodigal is painted about his bed, so FRESH and NEW that it must arrest attention, and well does he understand its meaning. Yet such a subject—such a lesson before his eyes when he is alone, and *should* come to himself, has no salutary effect upon him. " He that is froward, remains froward still."

Falstaff is a character from which we should derive more than mere amusement. A warning, indeed, it should be to those whose desires are well-nigh limited to gross pleasures and debasing objects.

ACT V. SCENE I.

A Room in the Garter Inn.
Dialogue between FORD, *who assumes the name of* BROOK, *and* SIR JOHN FALSTAFF.

"*Ford.* Went you not to her yesterday, sir, as you told me you had appointed?

Falstaff. I went to her, Master Brook, as you see, like a poor old man; but I came from her, Master Brook, like a poor old woman. That same knave, Ford her husband, hath the finest mad devil of jealousy in him, Master Brook, that ever governed frenzy. I will tell you. He beat me grievously in the shape of a woman; for in the shape of a man, Master Brook, *I fear not Goliath with a weaver's beam; because I know also, life is a shuttle.*"

In the present instance, a passage taken from historic narrative is blended with one taken from a moral reflection on the brevity and vanity of life: A smart bit of humour is the result.

["Goliath with a weaver's beam."]—" And there went out a champion out of the camp of the Philistines, named *Goliath* of Gath, whose height was six cubits and a span.

"And he had an helmet of brass upon his head, and he was armed with a coat of mail; and the weight of the coat was five thousand shekels of brass.

"And he had greaves of brass upon his legs, and a target of brass between his shoulders.

"*And the staff of his spear was like a weaver's beam;* and his spear's head weighed six hundred skekels of iron: and one bearing a shield went before him." 1 Sam. xvii. 4—7.

["Life is a shuttle."]—"My days are *swifter than a weaver's shuttle*, and are spent without hope." Job vii. 6.

ACT V.   SCENE V.

Another part of Windsor Park.
Enter PAGE, FORD, MRS. PAGE, MRS. FORD.
They lay hold on Falstaff.

"*Mrs. Page.* Why, Sir John, do you think, though we would thrust virtue out of our hearts by the head and shoulders, and have given ourselves without scruple to hell, that ever the devil could have made *you* our delight?

Ford. What, a hodge-pudding? a bag of flax?

Mrs. Page. A puff'd man?

Page. Old, cold, wither'd, and of intolerable entrails?

Ford. And one that is *as slanderous as Satan?*

Page. And as *poor as Job?*

Ford. And *as wicked as his wife.*"

In the first act and second scene of Henry IV., attention is arrested by the following example:—

Enter the LORD CHIEF JUSTICE *and* FALSTAFF.

" *Chief Justice.* To punish you by the heels, would amend the attention of your ears; and I care not if I do become your physician.

Falstaff. I am as poor as Job, my Lord; but not so patient."

["As slanderous as Satan, as poor as Job, as wicked as his wife."]—The extract from the second chapter of Job, which embraces these particulars, is somewhat long, though the *substance* of it is brought to our remembrance in *so few words* by means of dialogue:—

"And the Lord said unto Satan, Hast thou considered my servant Job, that there is none like him in the earth, a perfect and an upright man, one that feareth God, and escheweth evil? and still he holdeth fast his integrity, although thou movedst me against him, to destroy him without cause. And Satan answered the Lord, and said, Skin for skin, yea, all that a man hath will he give for his life.

"But put forth thine hand now, and touch his bone and his flesh, and he will curse thee to thy face.

"And the Lord said unto Satan, Behold, he is in thine hand; but save his life. So went Satan forth from the presence of the Lord, and smote Job with sore boils from the sole of his foot unto his crown.

"And he took him a potsherd to scrape himself withal; and he sat down among the ashes.

"Then said his wife unto him, Dost thou still retain thine integrity? Curse God, and die. But he said unto her, Thou speakest as one of the foolish women speaketh. What! shall we receive good at the hand of God, and shall we not receive evil? In all this did not Job sin with his lips." Job ii. 3—10.

In Troilus and Cressida, Anthony and Cleopatra, and Timon of Athens, Shakespeare's knowledge of the Bible is indicated; although these plays relate to historical matter concerning *heathen* nations.

CHAPTER XIII.

THE PLAY OF TROILUS AND CRESSIDA.

ACT I. SCENE III.

The Grecian Camp.

This passage, from a speech of Ulysses, is in a measure parallel with a passage which shall be produced from the 21st chapter of St. Luke's gospel.

"*Ulysses.* But when the planets,
In evil mixture, to disorder wander,
What plagues and what portents? what mutiny?
What raging of the sea? shaking of earth?
Commotions in the winds? frights, changes, horrors,
Divert and crack, rend and deracinate
The unity and married calm of states
Quite from their fixture?"

Quotation from St. Luke—

"And there shall be signs in the sun, and in the moon, and in the stars; and upon the earth distress of nations, with perplexity; the sea and the waves roaring; men's hearts failing them for fear, and for looking after those things which are coming on the earth: for the powers of heaven shall be shaken." Luke xxi. 25.

ACT I. SCENE III.

"*Æneas.* But peace, Æneas,
Peace, Trojan; lay thy finger on thy lips!
The worthiness of praise distains his worth,
If that the prais'd himself bring the praise forth."

In the 27th chapter of Proverbs we meet with the same sentiment:—

"Let another man praise thee, and not thine own mouth; a stranger, and not thine own lips." Prov. xvii. 2.

ACT II. SCENE II.

From Hector's answer to Paris and Troilus, who are both disposed to retain Helen:—

"*Hector.* Paris and Troilus, you have both said well:
And on the cause and question now on hand
Have gloz'd—but superficially; not much
Unlike young men, whom Aristotle thought
Unfit to hear moral philosophy:
The reasons you allege, do more conduce
To the hot passion of distemper'd blood,
Than to make up a free determination
'Twixt right and wrong; For pleasure and revenge

Have ears more deaf than adders to the voice
Of any true decision."

["Ears more deaf than adders."]—For this, Shakespeare seems indebted to the 4th and 5th verses of the 58th Psalm—

"Their poison is like the poison of a serpent: *they are like the deaf adder that stoppeth her ear;*
"*Which will not hearken to the voice of charmers*, charming never so wisely." Psalm lviii. 4, 5.

ACT III.   SCENE I.

Troy.

"*Pandarus.* Is this the generation of love? hot blood, hot thoughts, and hot deeds?—Why, *they are vipers:* Is love a *generation of vipers?*"

["Generation of vipers."]—There is the same form of expression in the 3rd chapter of St. Matthew—

"But when he saw many of the Pharisees and Sadducees come to his baptism, he said unto them, *O generation of vipers*, who hath warned you to flee from the wrath to come?" Matt. iii. 7.

The use of *Amen* by Pandarus, Troilus, and Cressida, is singular. Amen is, however, found in several plays which seem least to favour its admission—in Timon of Athens, for instance: it is found, too, in Cymbeline and Coriolanus.

CHAPTER XIV.

THE PLAY OF ANTHONY AND CLEOPATRA.

In this play, *Herod of Jewry* is several times to be met with. Herod is first mentioned in the dialogue between the Soothsayer and Charmian, one of Cleopatra's attendants.

ACT I. SCENE II.

"*Charmian.* Good now, some excellent fortune! Let me be married to three kings in a forenoon, and widow them all: let me have *a child at fifty, to whom Herod of Jewry may do homage.*"

Herod of Jewry was an Idumean by birth, but professed the Jewish religion. He was declared King of the Jews about thirty-eight years before our Lord was born at Bethlehem. He was afterwards called Herod the Great. The words of

Charmian, "*Let me have a child, to whom Herod of Jewry may do homage,*" seem in substance abstracted from a circumstance relative to Herod, that happened soon after the birth of Christ.

"Then Herod, when he had privily called the wise men, inquired of them diligently what time the star appeared.

"And he sent them to Bethlehem, and said, *Go and search diligently for the young child;* and when ye have found him, bring me word again, *that I may come and worship him also.*" Matt. ii. 7, 8.

The flight of Joseph with the Virgin Mary and the child Jesus into *Egypt*, that the child might not be destroyed by Herod; and—"that it might be fulfilled which was spoken of the Lord by the prophet, saying, *Out of Egypt* have I called my son"— might lead Shakespeare to put such words, connected with Herod's search for our Lord, into the mouth of Charmian, *an Egyptian*, with the sense which Steevens has given them:—" Charmian wishes for a son, who may arrive to such power and dominion that the proudest and fiercest monarchs of the earth may be brought under his yoke."

The addition of the word *fifty*—" Let me have a child at *fifty*, to whom Herod of Jewry may do homage," and the context, cover Shakespeare's retreat; but after research, cause the evidence, in favour of the *source* whence Shakespeare culled the notion, to be very presumptive.

Herod of Jewry is mentioned by Mistress Page in The Merry Wives of Windsor, in Act II., Scene I.

Before Page's House.

Enter MISTRESS PAGE *with Falstaff's Love-letter.*

"*Mistress Page.* What a *Herod of Jewry* is this! O, wicked, wicked world!"

She implies, doubtless, that Falstaff, like Herod, hesitates not to violate the most sacred bonds of love and friendship, in order to gain his own selfish ends.

But to return again to the play of Anthony and Cleopatra :—

ACT III. SCENE XI.

"*Cleopatra.* Wherefore is this?
Anthony. To let a fellow that will take rewards,
And say, God quit you! be familiar with
My playfellow, your hand; this kingly seal,
And plighter of high hearts! O that I were
Upon the hill of Basan, to outroar the horned herd!"

["Hill of Basan, to outroar the horned herd."]— "Many bulls have compassed me: strong bulls of Bashan have beset me round. They gaped upon me with their mouths, as a ravening and a roaring lion." Psalm xxii. 12, 13.

CHAPTER XV.

THE PLAY OF TIMON OF ATHENS.

The pertinent extracts about to be introduced, relate to Timon when reduced by his extreme liberality to penury: the first one refers to the ingratitude manifested by Lord Lucius when called on to assist his benefactor, now in the greatest distress.

ACT III. SCENE II.

"1st *Stranger.* Do you observe this Hostilius?
2nd *Stranger.* Ay, too well.
1st *Stranger.* Why, this is the world's sport;
And just of the same piece is every flatterer's soul.
Who can call him his friend
That dips in the same dish?"

["Who can call him friend that dips in the same dish?"]—Thoughts evidently borrowed from 23rd verse of 26th chapter of Matthew, where the Eastern mode of eating is mentioned.

" And he answered and said, *He that dippeth his hand with me in the dish,* the *same* shall *betray* me." Matt. xxvi. 23.

ACT V.   SCENE II.

The Woods.   Timon's Cave.

" *The Poet.* Then this breaking of his has been but a try for his friends?
The Painter. Nothing else: you shall *see him a palm* in Athens again, and *flourish* with the highest."

[" A palm and flourish."—The same sentiment is to be found in the 92nd Psalm :—

" *The righteous shall flourish like a palm-tree :* he shall grow like a cedar in Lebanon." Psalm xcii. 12.

CHAPTER XVI.

THE PLAY OF CORIOLANUS.

ACT II. SCENE I.

Rome.
Enter MENENIUS *with the Tribunes,* SICINIUS *and* BRUTUS.

"*Menenius.* The augurer tells me, we shall have news to-night.
Brutus. Good, or bad?
Menenius. Not according to the prayer of the people, for they love not Marcius.
Sicinius. Nature *teaches beasts to know their friends.*
Menenius. Pray you, *who does the wolf love?*
Sicinius. The lamb.
Menenius. Ay, *to devour him.*"

The ideas in italics seem borrowed from the 13th chapter of Ecclesiasticus.

"*Every beast loveth his like,* and every man loveth his neighbour.

"All flesh *consorteth according to kind*, and a man will cleave to his like.

"*What fellowship hath the wolf with the lamb?*" Ecclus. xiii. 15, 16, 17.

ACT II. SCENE I.

From the conference which the tribunes, Sicinius and Brutus, hold relative to Coriolanus:—

"*Brutus.*   For an end,
We must suggest the people in what hatred
He still hath held them. . . . . .
Sicinius. This, as you say, suggested
At some time when his soaring insolence
Shall reach the people (which time shall not want,
If he be put upon't; and that's as easy
As to set dogs on sheep), *will be the fire*
To *kindle their dry stubble;* and *their blaze*
Shall *darken him for ever.*"

["Will be *the fire* to *kindle their dry stubble;* and *their blaze* shall *darken him*," &c.]—A passage very parallel in metaphor to this, is to be found in the 18th verse of the book of the prophet Obadiah:—

"The house of Jacob *shall be a fire*, and the house of Joseph *a flame*, and *the house of Esau for stubble*, and *they shall kindle in them*, and devour them."

No instance important enough to warrant notice is to be found in Cymbeline; perhaps for this reason, because Shakespeare adheres literally to the details from which the subject was composed.

In the play of Julius Cæsar, the great master gives us very clear and correct notions of Roman manners; but, by confining himself strictly to the story, furnishes us with little connected with the object of our research.

ACT I.　SCENE II.

"*Cassius.* Therefore, good Brutus, be prepared to hear:
And, since you cannot see yourself
So well as by reflection, I, your glass,
Will modestly discover to yourself,
That of yourself which you yet know not of."

To the above there is a parallel in Proverbs:—

"As in water, face answereth to face, so the heart of man to man." Prov. xxvii. 19.

In the play of Othello, Shakespeare trammels his genius less than in the plays just noticed; if several pertinent examples may be considered sufficient evidence for such conclusion.

ACT IV.　SCENE II.

Another Apartment in the Castle.

"*Æmilia.* I durst, my lord, to wager she is honest,
Lay down my soul at stake: if you think other,
Remove your thought; it doth abuse your bosom.

If any wretch hath put this in your head,
Let heaven requite it with the serpent's curse!"

Æmilia, the wife of Iago, endeavours thus to persuade Othello that Desdemona is indeed as virtuous as he would fain believe her to be.

[" Let heaven requite it with the serpent's curse."—
" Let him suffer at once *the curse which the serpent brought upon man*—viz., death: may he be visited with instant death, whoever invented so wicked a lie!"]

[" Serpent's curse."]—" And the woman said unto the serpent, we may eat of the fruit of the trees of the garden:

" But of the fruit of the tree which is in the midst of the garden, God hath said, *Ye shall not eat of it, neither shall ye touch it, lest ye die.*

" And the *serpent said* unto the woman, *Ye shall not surely die:* for God doth know that in the day ye eat thereof, then your eyes shall be opened, and ye shall be as gods, knowing good and evil." Gen. iii. 2—5.

Æmilia fails, however, to eradicate the fatal jealousy which poisons the Moor's mind, and drinks up his spirit; for, says Othello—

" Had it pleased Heaven
   To try me with affliction; had it rain'd
   All kinds of sores, and shames, on my bare head;
   Steep'd me in poverty to the very lips;
   Given to captivity me and my utmost hopes;
   I should have found in some place of my soul
   A drop of patience."

For the substance of these lines, Shakespeare appears to be indebted to the 1st and 2nd chapters of Job. Thus :—

["All kinds of sores and shames on my bare head."]—" And the Lord said unto Satan, Behold, he is in thine hand ; but save his life.

" So went Satan forth from the presence of the Lord, and smote Job *with sore boils from the sole of his foot unto his crown.*" Job ii. 6, 7.

Thus, again :—

[" Steep'd me in poverty to the very lips ; given to captivity me and my utmost hopes."]—" And the Lord said unto Satan, Behold, all that he hath is in thy power ;

"And there came a messenger unto Job, and said, The oxen were ploughing, and the asses feeding beside them :

" And the *Sabeans fell upon them,* and *took them away;* yea, *they have slain the servants with the edge of the sword ;* and I only am escaped alone to tell thee.

" While he was yet speaking, there came also another, and said, *The fire of God is fallen from heaven, and hath burned up the sheep, and the servants, and consumed them ;* and I only am escaped alone to tell thee.

" While he was yet speaking, there came also another, and said, *The Chaldeans made out three bands, and fell upon the camels, and have carried them away, yea, and slain the servants with the edge of the sword ;* and I only am escaped alone to tell thee." Job i. 12—17.

Othello. The same speech continued—

" But there, where I have garner'd up my heart;
Where either I must live, or bear no life;
The *fountain* from which my current runs,
Or else dries up, to be discarded thence;
Or keep it *as a cistern* for foul toads," &c.

In the lines just quoted, Othello speaks of his wife as a *fountain*—a *cistern* : expressions which we shall again have occasion to notice hereafter. The expressions a *fountain*—a *cistern*—may be taken in the present instance from Prov. v. 15, 18.

" Drink waters out of *thine own cistern*, and running waters out of thine own well.

" Let *thy fountains* be dispersed abroad, and rivers of waters in the streets.

" Let them be *only thine own*, and *not strangers with thee*.

" Let thy *fountain* be blessed : and rejoice with the wife of thy youth." Prov. v. 15—18.

CHAPTER XVII.

THE PLAY OF THE TEMPEST.

ACT I. SCENE II.

The Characters. Prospero, an inhabitant of the enchanted island, but the rightful Duke of Milan, and the monster Caliban.

"*Caliban.* I must eat my dinner.
This island's mine, by Sycorax my mother,
Which thou tak'st from me.   When thou cam'st first,
Thou stroak'st me, and mad'st much of me; would'st
      give me
Water with berries in't; and teach me how
To name the bigger light, and how the less,
That burn by day and night; and then I lov'd thee,
And show'd thee all the qualities o' the isle,
The fresh springs, brine-pits, barren place, and fertile;
Curs'd be I that I did so!   All the charms
Of Sycorax, toads, beetles, bats, light on you,

For I am all the subjects that you have,
Who first was mine own king : and here you sty me
In this hard rock, whiles you do keep from me
The rest of the island."

["To name the bigger light."]—This is evidently taken from Gen. i. 16.

"*And God made two great lights; the greater light to rule the day, and the lesser light to rule the night : he made the stars also.*" Gen. i. 16.

"*Prospero.* Thou most lying slave,
Whom stripes may move, not kindness: I have used thee,
Filth as thou art, with human care; and lodg'd thee
In mine own cell, till thou did'st seek to violate
The honour of my child."

We here quote thus fully that the character of Caliban may be known, and the reader be thus prepared for the example in the third act, which owes much of its point to this uncouth monster.

ACT III. SCENE II.

Caliban plots against Prospero's life.

"*Caliban.* I say by sorcery he got this isle ;
From me he got it. If thy greatness will
Revenge it on him [for I know thou dar'st,
But this thing dare not "—]

These words are addressed to Stephano, a drunken butler, who has made Caliban drunk.

" *Stephano.* That's most certain.
Caliban. Thou shalt be lord of it, and I'll serve thee.
Stephano. How now shall this be compass'd? Canst thou bring me to the party?
Caliban. Yea, yea, my lord ; *I'll yield him thee asleep, Where thou may'st knock a nail into his head.*"

["I'll yield him thee asleep, where thou may'st knock a nail into his head."]—In Judges iv., we find that Sisera, captain of the host of Jabin, king of Canaan, when discomfited by Israel, fled away on his feet to a tent for safety, but was there put to death in the manner devised by Caliban.

[Death of Sisera, captain of Jabin's host.]—" Then Jael, Heber's wife, *took a nail of the tent,* and took a hammer in her hand, and went softly unto him, and *smote the nail into his temples, and fastened it into the ground : for he was fast asleep and weary. So he died.*

" And behold, as Barak pursued Sisera, Jael came out to meet him, and said unto him, Come, I will show you the man whom thou seekest.

" And when he came into her tent, behold Sisera lay dead, *and the nail was in his temples.*" Judges iv. 21, 22.

ACT V. SCENE I.

["Thy dukedom I resign."]—The duchy of Milan being, through the treachery of Anthonio (Prospero's brother), made feudatory to the crown of Naples, Alonso promises to resign his claim of sovereignty for the future. *Steevens.*

"*Alonso.* Thy dukedom I resign, and do entreat
Thou pardon me my wrongs; but how should Prospero
Be living, and be here?
   Prospero. First, noble friend,
Let me embrace thine age; whose honour cannot
Be measur'd or confin'd.
   Gonzalo. Whether this be,
Or be not, I'll not swear.
   Prospero. You do yet taste
Some subtilties o' the isle, that will not let you
Believe things certain: Welcome, my friends all;
But you, my brace of lords, were I so minded,
          (*Aside to Sebastian and Anthonio*)
I here could pluck his highness' frown upon you,
And justify you traitors; at this time
I'll tell no tales."

[*Sebastian.* "*The devil speaks in him.*"]—Shakespeare might abstract this notion, which in few words expresses so much, from such a passage of Scripture as this—

"And he healed many that were sick of divers diseases, and cast out many devils, and suffered not *the devils to speak*, because they knew him." Mark i. 34.

Amen occurs twice in the fifth act of the Tempest; it is put in the mouth of the drunken Stephano—Thus, in act 2nd, scene 2nd—

"*Stephano.* If all the wine in my bottle will recover him, I will help his ague: come, *Amen !*"

In the Midsummer Night's Dream, *Amen* is

introduced in such a way as to indicate the *exclusive* use to which it should be applied.

ACT II.   SCENE III.

"*Lysander. Amen, Amen,* to that *fair prayer,* say I."

So also in Macbeth is the same thing noticeable.

" One cried, *God bless us!* and *Amen* the other; I could not say *Amen,* when they did say *God bless us!* * * I had most need of *blessing,* and *Amen* stuck in my throat."

CHAPTER XVII.

MIDSUMMER NIGHT'S DREAM.

ACT III. SCENE II.

"*Hermia. An adder did it;* for with doubler tongue Than *thine, thou serpent, never adder stung.*"

["An adder did it."]—The play of King Lear furnishes us with a similar form of expression.

"*Lear.* Struck me *with her tongue, most serpent-like, upon the very heart.*"

Both plays derive the idea from the same source, it appears—viz., 140th Psalm.

"They have *sharpened their tongues like a serpent; adder's poison is under their lips.*" Psalm cxl. 3.

Another sentence in Lear, parallel with a verse in this Psalm, confirms this opinion.

"*Lear.* All the stored vengeances of heaven fall on her ingrateful top."

The 140th Psalm—

"As for the head of those that compass me about, let the mischief of their own lips cover them." Psalm cxl. 9.

The play of King Lear contains one more example; where the King is deserted, because he is in adversity, by many of those who were his attendants.

ACT II. SCENE IV.

"*Kent.* How chance the king comes with so small a train?
Fool. An thou hadst been set i' the stocks for that question, thou hadst well deserv'd it.
Kent. Why, fool?
Fool. We'll *set thee to school to an ant,* to teach thee *there's no labouring in the winter.*"

["Set thee to school to an ant," &c.]—Either from Proverbs vi. 6, 7, 8—

"Go to the ant, thou sluggard; consider her ways, and be wise:
"Which having no guide, overseer, or ruler, *provideth her meat in the summer,* and *gathereth her food in the harvest.*"

Or, Proverbs xxx. 25—

"The ants are a people not strong, yet they prepare their meat in the summer."

K

The evidence from the play of Romeo and Juliet, in which the Montagues and Capulets, two hostile families, are brought together by a common calamity, is not unimportant, though it may have been hitherto unnoticed.

ACT I.   SCENE III.

A Room in Capulet's House.   Enter LADY CAPULET *and* NURSE.

"*Lady Cap.* Nurse, where's my daughter? call her forth to me.
Nurse. Now, by my maidenhead at twelve year old,
I bade her come.—What, lamb! what, lady bird!
God forbid!—where's this girl?—what, Juliet!"

It may be presumed that Shakespeare, when he uses the expression *God forbid*, adopts St. Paul's strong form of deprecation. When Measure for Measure is introduced, *God forbid* will be found in the passage from the 9th chapter of St. Paul's Epistle to the Romans, which we shall then have occasion to quote.

FROM ACT II.   SCENE II.

"*Juliet.*   Romeo, doff thy name;
And for that name, which is no part of thee,
Take all myself.

Romeo. I take thee at thy word :
Call me but love, and *I'll be new baptized.*"

["Be new baptized."]—With such knowledge of Holy Writ as Shakespeare had, it is not surprising that thoughts derived from certain passages therein should involuntarily arise in his mind.

Shakespeare was for instance well versed in all such passages as these :—

"*I indeed baptize you* with water unto repentance : but he that cometh after me . . . . . . he *shall baptize* you," &c. Matt. iii. 11.

"For John truly *baptized* with water ; but ye *shall be baptized,* &c. . . not many days hence." Acts i. 5.

Again, also, from

ACT II. SCENE II.

"*Romeo.* What shall I swear by ?
Juliet. Do not swear at all ;
Or, if thou wilt, *swear by thy gracious self,*
Which is the god of my idolatry,
And I'll believe thee."

Shakespeare seems indebted for this striking form of expression—

"*Swear by thy gracious self, which is the god,*" &c.—

to the 6th chapter of Hebrews, 13th verse; it is there stated—

"When God made promise to Abraham, because *he could swear by no greater, he sware by himself.*"

But he has contrived, notwithstanding this suspicious circumstance, to keep the proper train of thought in the reader's mind—"Swear by thy gracious self;" *i. e.*, Promise me, beloved one, that you will indeed be true to me. The passage may be said to glow with the youthful fervour of pure affection.

ACT II. SCENE VI.

Friar Lawrence's Cell. The FRIAR *and* ROMEO.

"*Romeo.* Do thou but close our hands with holy words,
Then love-devouring death do what he dare,
It is enough I may but call her mine.
Friar. These violent delights have violent ends,
And in their triumph die; like fire and powder,
Which, as they kiss, consume : *The sweetest honey
Is loathsome in his own deliciousness*,
And in the taste confounds the appetite :
Therefore, love moderately; long love doth so ;
Too swift arrives as tardy as too slow."

["The sweetest honey is loathsome," &c.]— In the Proverbs there is a passage to the same effect—

" Hast thou found honey? eat so much as is sufficient for thee, lest thou be filled therewith, and vomit it." Prov. xxv. 16.

TWELFTH NIGHT; OR, WHAT YOU WILL.

The rich and beautiful Olivia, beloved by the Duke Orsino, takes a fancy to Viola, a lady who loves the Duke, but is ostensibly his page. Finally, mistakes are rectified; Sebastian, Viola's long-lost brother, marries Olivia; and Viola becomes the wife of Orsino.

Our examples from this play do not belong to any of these leading characters; but are no mean additions to the evidence already collected.

ACT I. SCENE V.

Enter MARIA *and* CLOWN.

"*Maria.* You are resolute, then?

Clown. Not so neither; but I am resolv'd on two points.

Maria. That if one break, the other will hold; or, if both break, your gaskins fall.

Clown. Apt in good faith; very apt! Well, go thy way; if Sir Toby would leave drinking, thou wert as witty *a piece of Eve's flesh* as any in Illyria."

["A piece of Eve's flesh."]—A humorous deduction from the 20th verse of the 3rd chapter of Genesis—

"And Adam called his wife's name *Eve;* because she was *the mother of all living.*"

ACT II. SCENE V.

Malvolio, a fantastical steward to Olivia, is induced to believe that this lady loves him, by a letter which Maria, her woman, throws in his way.

"*Malvolio.* There is example for't; the lady of the strachy married the yeoman of the wardrobe.
Sir Andrew (*who in ambush hears this soliloquy*). Fie on him, Jezebel!"

["*Jezebel.*"]—Sir Andrew, who says this, is of weak intellect. We shall hereafter have occasion to speak particularly of *Jezebel* and Ahab: the 1st Book of Kings furnishes us with their history. Again—

ACT II. SCENE V.

Enter MARIA, *who has been gulling* MALVOLIO.

"*Sir Toby.* I could marry the wench for this device.
Sir Andrew. So could I, too.
Sir Toby. And ask no other dowry with her but such another jest.
Sir Andrew. Nor I neither.
Fabian. Here comes my noble gull-catcher.
Sir Toby. Wilt thou set thy foot o' my neck?
Sir Andrew. Or o' mine either?"

This seems traceable to a passage in the 10th chapter of Joshua—

"And it came to pass, when they brought out those kings unto Joshua, that Joshua called for all the men of Israel, and said unto the captains of the men of war which went with him, Come near, *put your feet upon the necks of these kings.* And they came near, *and put their feet upon the necks of them.*" Josh. x. 24.

Words to this effect are put into the mouth of Volumnia, in the third scene and first act of the play, entitled " Coriolanus :"—

"*Volum.* He'll beat Aufidius' head below his knee, *And tread upon his neck.*"

ACT III. SCENE II.

"*Fabian.* I will prove it legitimate, sir, by the oaths of judgment and reason.

Sir Toby. And they have been grand-jurymen since *before Noah was a sailor.*"

["Before Noah was a sailor."]—Shakespeare may derive this allusion to the deluge, either from the 7th chapter of Genesis—the 3rd chapter of the 1st Epistle of St. Peter—or the 2nd chapter of the 2nd Epistle of this writer. There are two more extracts from plays which contain allusions to the deluge; one in As You Like It, and another in the Comedy of Errors. These cases shall be here brought together, followed by a pertinent passage from the Book of Genesis.

CHAPTER XVIII.

AS YOU LIKE IT.

ACT V. SCENE IV.

Enter TOUCHSTONE *and* AUDREY.

"*Jacques.* There is, sure, *another flood toward, and these couples are coming to the ark!* Here comes a pair of very strange beasts, which in all tongues are called fools."

CHAPTER XIX.

THE COMEDY OF ERRORS.
ACT III.   SCENE II.

"*Antip. of Syracuse.* What complexion is she of ?
Dromio of Syracuse. Swart, like my shoe, but her face nothing like so clean kept; for why? she sweats, a man may go over his shoes in the grime of it.
Antip. of Syracuse. That's a fault that water will mend.
Dromio of Syracuse. No, sir, 'tis in grain; *Noah's flood* could not do it."

["Noah's flood," &c.]—"And the rain was upon the earth forty days and forty nights. In the selfsame day entered Noah, and Shem, and Ham, and Japheth, the sons of Noah, and Noah's wife, and the three wives of his sons with them, into the ark;
"They, and *every beast after his kind*, and all the cattle after their kind, and every creeping thing that creepeth upon the earth after his kind, and every fowl after his kind, every bird of every sort. And *they went in unto Noah into the ark, two and two of all flesh*, wherein is the breath of life.
" And *the flood was forty days upon the earth ;* and the waters increased, *and bare up the ark*, and it was lift up above the earth." 'Gen. vii. 12—15, 17.

CHAPTER XX.

TWELFTH NIGHT.

ACT III. SCENE IV.

"*Sir Toby.* Which way is he, in the name of sanctity?
If *all the devils of hell be drawn in little,*
And *Legion himself possess'd him*, yet I'll speak to him."

["The devils be drawn in little, and Legion himself possess'd him."]—For this strong language, applied to Malvolio, because he had been making himself ridiculous before Olivia, see the 30th verse of 8th chapter of St. Luke:—

"What is thy name? and he said, *Legion: because many devils were entered into him.*"

The 9th verse of the 5th chapter of St. Mark is very similar to the one here put down.

ACT V. SCENE I.

The CLOWN *derides* MALVOLIO'S *passion for* OLIVIA.

"*Clown.* Truly, madam, he holds *Belzebub* at the stave's end, as well as any man in his case may do: h'as here writ a letter to you, I should have given't you to-day morning; but, as *a madman's epistles are no gospels,* so it skills not much when they are delivered.
Olivia. Open't, and read it."

St. Paul, from whose writings our poet selects passages, is declared by Festus *to be mad* :—

"Paul, thou art beside thyself; much learning *doth make thee mad.*
"But he said, I am *not mad,* most noble Festus, but speak forth the words of truth and soberness." Acts xxvi. 24, 25.

This false charge against St. Paul, and the peculiar circumstances which call forth Malvolio's epistle, might give rise to the humorous remark— *A madman's epistles are no gospels.*

CHAPTER XXI.

THE TWO GENTLEMEN OF VERONA.

Launce and Speed, the awkward servants of the two gentlemen, Proteus and Valentine, furnish minor additions to the matter now before us.

ACT II. SCENE V.

"*Speed.* But tell me true, will't be a match?

Launce. Ask my dog: if he say Ay, it will; if he say No, it will; if he shake his tail and say nothing, it will.

Speed. The conclusion is, then, that it will.

Launce. Thou shalt never get such a secret from me, *but by a parable.*"

["But by a parable."]—"*Without a parable* spake he not unto them." Matt. xiii. 34.

"I will open my mouth in a parable." Psalm lxxviii. 2.

ACT II. SCENE V.

"*Speed.* I tell thee my master is become a hot lover.
Launce. Why, I tell thee, I care not though he burn himself in love. If thou wilt go with me to the ale-house, so; if not, thou art an *Hebrew*, a *Jew*, not worth the name of a *Christian*.
Speed. Why?
Launce. Because thou hast not so much charity in thee as to go to the ale-house with a *Christian*."

["If not, thou art an Hebrew, a Jew."]—A playful allusion, perhaps, to the prejudices of the first Jewish Christians, of which we subjoin an instance:—

"And when Peter was come up to Jerusalem, they that were of the circumcision contended with him, saying,
"Thou wentest in to men uncircumcised, and didst eat with them." Acts xi. 2, 3.

ACT III. SCENE I.

"*Speed.* Item. She is *proud*.
Launce. Out with that too; it was *Eve's legacy*, and cannot be taken from her."

["Pride, Eve's legacy."]—From this passage—
"When the woman saw that the tree was good for food, and that it was pleasant to the eyes, *and a tree*

to be desired to make one wise, she took of the fruit thereof." Gen. iii. 6.

We now pass on to The Merchant of Venice; from this play we aggregate impressive evidence of Shakespeare's biblical lore :—

ACT I. SCENE III.

"*Shylock.* But ships are but boards, sailors but men : there be land rats and water rats, water thieves and land thieves—I mean pirates ; and then there is the peril of waters, winds, and rocks. The man (Anthonio) is notwithstanding sufficient :—three thousand ducats ;—I think I may take his bond.

Bassanio. Be assur'd you may.

Shylock. I will be assur'd I may ; and, that I may be assur'd, I will bethink me. May I speak with Anthonio ?

Bassanio. If it please you to dine with us.

Shylock. Yes, to smell pork ; *to eat of the habitation which your prophet the Nazarite conjured the devil into:* I will buy with you, sell with you, talk with you, walk with you, and so following ; but I will not eat with you, drink with you, nor pray with you."

["To eat of that which your prophet the Nazarite."]—The word *Nazarite,* in this instance, merely means *Nazarene,* or inhabitant of Nazareth, a town of Galilee. Our Saviour was despised and rejected by the Jews, because he was conceived and brought up at Nazareth. The ill name which Nazareth had amongst the Jews, is clear from the following extract—

" Philip findeth Nathaniel, and saith unto him, We have found him of whom Moses in the law, and the prophets, did write, *Jesus of Nazareth*, the son of Joseph. And Nathaniel said unto him, *Can any good thing come out of Nazareth ?* Philip saith unto him, Come and see." John i. 45, 46.

Samson and Samuel were *Nazarites* in a different sense. The word Nazarite, applied to these characters, denotes a particular sort of separation and devotedness to God. The Nazarite was "to drink no wine nor strong drink, and to let no razor touch his head," in token of this separation. Of these Nazarites there were two kinds: those who were devoted to God for life; and those who were Nazarites only for a limited time. Samson and Samuel belonged to the former kind, which was, in some respects, lest strict than the latter.

[" Your prophet the Nazarite conjured the devil into."]—This miracle is recorded in the 8th chapter of St. Luke—

" And they arrived at the country of the Gadarenes, which is over against Galilee. And when he went forth to land, there met him out of the city a certain man which had devils long time, and ware no clothes, neither abode in any house, but in the tombs.

" When he saw Jesus, he cried out, and fell down

before him, and with a loud voice said, What have I to do with thee, Jesus, thou son of God Most High? I beseech thee, torment me not. (For he had commanded *the unclean spirit* to come out of the man.) And Jesus asked *him,* saying, What is thy name? And *he said,* Legion : because many devils were entered into him.

" And they besought him that he would not command them to go out into the deep.

" And there was there *an herd of many swine* feeding on the mountain : and they besought him *that he would suffer them to enter into them. And he suffered them.*

" *Then went the devils out of the man, and entered into the swine :* and the herd ran violently down a steep place into the lake, and were choked." Luke viii. 26—33.

As Shylock says, however, in reference to this miracle, " conjured the *devil* into," *not devils ;* the thought might arise from the account given in the 5th chapter of St. Mark : the parable there ends thus—

" And they come to Jesus, and see him which was possessed with *the devil,* and had *the legion,* sitting, and clothed, and in his right mind : and they were afraid.

" And they that saw it told them how it befell to him that was possessed with *the devil,* and also *concerning the swine.* And they began to pray him to depart out of their coasts.

"And when he was come into the ship, he that had been possessed with *the devil* prayed him that he might be with him." Mark v. 15—18.

ACT I. SCENE III.

"*Shylock.* What news on the Rialto ? Who is he comes here ?

Enter ANTHONIO.

Bassanio. This is signior Anthonio.
Shylock (aside). How like *a fawning publican* he looks !
I hate him for he is a *Christian.*"

["A fawning publican he looks."]—Such a temper is shown in three extracts which we will produce, e. g.—

" Why eateth your master with *publicans* and sinners ?" Mat. ix. 11.

" Why do ye eat and drink with *publicans* and sinners ?" Luke v. 30.

And again, in the Pharisee's prayer to the Most High—

" I thank thee, that I am not as other men are, extortioners, unjust, adulterers, or *even as this publican.*" Luke xviii. 11.

But we cannot *determine* from what source the notion, " How like a fawning *publican* he looks," without doubt, comes.

["I hate him for he is a *Christian.*"]—On the supposition that the notion "*fawning publican*" was taken from any or all of the passages above

L

quoted, the term *Christian* would still be correct in Shylock's mouth; for Shylock may be said to live now. The word Christian was not known till after our Lord's departure from the world: our proof of this is negative in the Gospels, but positive in the Acts of the Apostles: "The disciples were called *Christians* first at Antioch." Acts xi. 26.

ACT I. SCENE III.

"*Shylock*. When Jacob grazed his uncle Laban's sheep,
This Jacob from our holy Abraham was
(As his wise mother wrought in his behalf)
The third possessor; ay, he *was the third.*"

["As his wise mother wrought in his behalf—the third possessor."]—Jacob, instigated by his mother, Rebekah, obtains from Isaac, his father, the blessing designed for the first-born Esau. He obtains from Esau his birthright; and consequently gains both the birthright and the blessing. He was, as Shylock states, inheritor of the promise which had been made by the Most High to Abraham and to his son Isaac.

"And Rebekah spake unto Jacob her son, saying, Behold, I heard thy father speak unto Esau thy brother, saying,

"Bring me venison and make me savoury meat, that I may eat, and bless thee before the Lord before my death.

"Now therefore, my son, *obey my voice according to that which I command thee.* Go now to the flock, and fetch me from thence two good kids of the goats; and I will make them savoury meat for thy father, such as he loveth: and thou shalt bring it to thy father, that he may eat, and that he may bless thee before his death. And Jacob said unto Rebekah his mother, Behold, Esau my brother is a hairy man, and I am a smooth man.

"My father peradventure will feel me, and I shall seem to him as a deceiver; and I shall bring a curse upon me, and not a blessing.

"And *his mother said unto him,* Upon me be thy curse, my son: *only obey my voice, and go fetch me them.*" Gen. xxvii. 6—12.

We know, too, what follows—Rebekah put goodly raiment of her son Esau upon Jacob, and put the skins of the goats upon his hands and upon the smooth of his neck, and dressed for him savoury meat such as Isaac loved. The device was successful: yet the blind and infirm Isaac was not easily deceived; for after examination he says to Jacob—

"The voice is Jacob's voice, but the hands are the hands of Esau."

He also adds even then—

"Art thou my very son Esau? and he said, I am."

Isaac then partakes of the savoury meat brought by Jacob, and blesses him in these words—

"God give thee of the dew of heaven, and the fatness of the earth, and plenty of corn and wine.

"Let people serve thee, and nations bow down to thee: be lord over thy brethren, and let thy mother's sons bow down to thee: cursed be every one that curseth thee, and blessed be he that blesseth thee." Gen. xxvii. 28, 29.

"*Antonio.* And what of him; did he [*i. e., Jacob*] take interest?

Shylock. No, not take interest; not, as you would say, Directly interest: mark what Jacob did.
When *Laban and himself were compromis'd,*
That all the eanlings which were streak'd and pied
Should fall, as Jacob's hire; the ewes, being rank
In the end of autumn, turned to the rams:
And when the work of generation was
Between these woolly breeders in the act,
The skilful shepherd peel'd me certain wands,
And in the doing of the deed of kind,
He stuck them up before the fulsome ewes;
Who, then conceiving, did in eaning time
Fall party-coloured lambs, and those were Jacob's.
This was a way to thrive, and he was blest;
And thrift is blessing, if men steal it not."

["The skilful shepherd peel'd me certain wands."]—
"And Laban said unto him, I pray thee, if I have found favour in thine eyes, tarry: . . . . .

"And he said, Appoint me thy wages, and I will give it.

"And he said, What shall I give thee? and Jacob said, Thou shalt not give me any thing: if thou wilt do this thing for me, I will again feed and keep thy flock.

"I will pass through all thy flock to-day, removing from thence all the speckled and spotted cattle, and all the brown cattle amongst the sheep, and the spotted and speckled among the goats: and of such shall be my hire.

"So shall my righteousness answer for me in time to come, when it shall come for my hire before thy face: every one that *is not speckled and spotted* among the *goats,* and *brown among the sheep, that shall be counted stolen with me.*

"And Laban said, Behold, I would it might be according to thy word.

"And he *removed* that day the *he-goats that were ring-straked and spotted,* and *all the she-goats that were speckled and spotted,* and *every one* that had *some white in it,* and *all the brown among the sheep,* and gave them into the hand of his sons.

"And he set three days' journey betwixt himself and Jacob: and Jacob fed the rest of Laban's flocks.

"And Jacob *took him rods of green poplar,* and of the hazel and chestnut tree ; and *pilled white strakes in them,* and *made the white appear which was in the rods.*

"And he set *the rods which he had pilled before the flocks* in the gutters, in the watering-troughs when the flocks came to drink, that they should conceive when they came to drink.

"And *the flocks conceived before the rods, and brought forth cattle ring-straked, speckled, and spotted.*

"And Jacob did separate the lambs, and *set the faces of the flocks toward the ring-straked,* and all the brown in the flock of Laban; and he put his own flocks by themselves, and put them not unto Laban's cattle.

"And it came to pass, whenever the *stronger cattle did conceive*, that Jacob *laid the rods before the eyes of the cattle* in the gutters, that they might *conceive among the rods.*

"But when the cattle were feeble, he put them not in: so the feebler were Laban's and the stronger Jacob's." Gen. xxx. 27-42.

Anthonio then adds in answer to Shylock—

"*Anthonio.* This was a venture, sir, that Jacob served for;
A thing not in his power to bring to pass,
But sway'd, and fashion'd, by the hand of Heaven.
Was this inserted to make interest good?
Or is your gold and silver, ewes and rams?
 Shylock. I cannot tell; I make it breed as fast:—
But note me, signior.
 Anthonio. Mark you this, Bassanio,
The devil can cite scripture for his purpose."

Satan cites scripture for his purpose in 4th chapter of Matthew, when he says to Christ—"If thou be the Son of God, cast thyself down [from this pinnacle of the temple]; for it is written, "He shall give his angels charge concerning thee: and in their hands they shall bear thee up, lest at any time thou dash thy foot against a stone." See 11th and 12th verses of 91st Psalm.

["A thing not in his power to bring to pass, but

sway'd, and fashion'd, by the hand of Heaven."]—" And Jacob beheld the countenance of Laban, and, beheld, it was not towards him as before.

"And the Lord said unto Jacob, Return unto the land of thy fathers, and to thy kindred; and I will be with thee.

" And Jacob sent and called Rachel and Leah to the field unto his flock.

"And said unto them, I see your father's countenance, that it is not toward me as before; but the God of my father hath been with me.

" And ye know, that with all my power I have served your father.

" And your father hath deceived me, and changed my wages ten times; but God suffered him not to hurt me.

"If he said thus, The *speckled* shall be thy wages; then all the cattle bare *speckled:* and if he said thus, *The ring-straked* shall be thy hire; then bare all the cattle *ring-straked.*

"Thus God hath taken away the cattle of your father, and given them to me." Gen. xxxi. 2—9.

ACT II. SCENE V.

Shylock's House. Enter SHYLOCK *and* LAUNCELOT, *and then* JESSICA.

"*Shylock.* What! are there masques? Hear you me, Jessica:
Lock up my doors; and when you hear the drum,
And the vile squeaking of the wry-neck'd fife,

Clamber not you up to the casements then,
Nor thrust your head into the public street,
To gaze on Christian fools with varnish'd faces :
But stop my house's ears, I mean my casements ;
Let not the sound of shallow foppery enter
My sober house.—By *Jacob's staff, I swear*,
I have no mind of feasting forth to-night:
But I will go.—Go you before me, sirrah ;
Say I will come.

    Launcelot. I will go before, sir.—
Mistress, look out at window, for all this ;
    There will come a Christian by,
    Will be worth a Jewess' eye.
    Shylock. What says that fool of *Hagar's offspring*, ha ?
    Jessica. His words were, Farewell, mistress ; nothing else."

["By Jacob's staff, I swear."]—By a *word* sometimes, Shakespeare shows how thoroughly he must have read the Bible. Jacob mentions *his staff* in the 10th verse of the 32nd chapter of Genesis.

"And Jacob said, O God of my father Abraham, and God of my father Isaac, the Lord which saidst unto me, Return unto thy country, and to thy kindred, and I will deal well with thee :

"I am not worthy of the least of all the mercies, and of all the truth, which thou hast shewed unto thy servant ; *for with my staff I passed over this Jordan ; and now I am become two bands.*" Gen. xxxii. 9, 10.

["That fool of *Hagar's* offspring."]—"And Sarah

saw the son of *Hagar* the Egyptian, which she had born unto Abraham, mocking.

"Wherefore she said unto Abraham, Cast out this bondwoman and her son:—And God said unto Abraham, let it not be grievous in thy sight because of the lad, and because of thy bondwoman; in all that Sarah hath said unto thee, hearken unto her voice; for in Isaac shall thy seed be called.

"And also of the son of the bondwoman will I make a nation, because he is thy seed." Gen. xxi. 9, 10—12, 13.

ACT III. SCENE I.

A Street in Venice.

"*Tubal.* There came divers of Anthonio's creditors in my company to Venice, that swear he cannot chuse but break.

Shylock. I am glad of it; I'll plague him; I'll torture him; I am glad of it.

Tubal. One of them showed me a ring, that he had of your daughter for a monkey.

Shylock. Out upon her! Thou torturest me, *Tubal:* it was my torquoise; I had it of *Leah,* when I was a bachelor: I would not have given it for a wilderness of monkeys."

Leah and *Tubal* are both names found in scripture; we have already quoted passages which contain them. *Leah* is found in a passage quoted in this play, and *Tubal* in one quoted in the play of Henry IV.

["Tubal."]—"The sons of Japheth; Gomer, and Magog, and Madai, and Javan, and *Tubal.* Gen. x. 2.

ACT III.   SCENE V.

Enter LAUNCELOT *and* JESSICA.

"*Launcelot.* Yes, truly;—for, look you, *the sins of the father are to be laid upon the children;* therefore, I promise you, I fear you."

["Sins of the father to be laid upon the children."]— "Visiting the iniquity of the fathers upon the children unto the third and fourth generation of them that hate me." Exodus xx. 5.

ACT IV.   SCENE I.

"*Shylock.* These be the Christian husbands : I have a daughter—
'Would any of *the stock of Barrabas*
Had been her husband, rather than a Christian!"
(*Aside.*)

Shylock thus mutters to himself, when Bassanio and Gratiano protest that they would sacrifice their wives, dear as they are to them, to deliver Anthonio from his implacable enemy. These words of Shylock are, of necessity, introduced before matter which, in the play, will be found to precede them.

["The stock of Barrabas or Barabbas."]—"They had then a *notable prisoner, called Barabbas.*

"The chief priests and elders persuaded the multitude that they should *ask Barabbas, and destroy Jesus*.

"The governor answered and said unto them, Whether of the twain will ye that I release unto you? They said, *Barabbas*." Matt. xxvii. 16, 20, 21.

"They cried out all at once, saying, Away with this man, and *release unto us Barabbas:*

("Who *for a certain sedition* made in the city, *and for murder*, was cast into prison." Luke xxiii. 18, 19.

"Then cried they all again, saying, [release] Not this man, *but Barabbas.* Now *Barabbas was a robber.*" John xviii. 40.

ACT IV. SCENE I.

"*Portia.* Do you confess the bond?
Anthonio. I do.
Portia. Then must the Jew be merciful.
Shylock. On what compulsion must I? tell me that.
Portia. The quality of mercy is not strained;
It droppeth, *as the gentle rain from heaven*
Upon the place beneath: *it is twice bless'd;*
It blesseth him that gives, and him that takes:
'Tis mightiest in the mightiest; it becomes
The throned *monarch* better than his *crown:*
His sceptre shews the force of temporal power,
The attribute to awe and majesty,
Wherein doth sit the dread and fear of kings;
But mercy is above this sceptr'd sway,
It is enthroned in the hearts of kings,
It is an attribute to God himself;

And earthly power doth *then shew likest God's,*
When *mercy seasons justice :* Therefore, Jew,
Though justice be thy plea, consider this,—
That *in the course of justice, none of us
Should see salvation : we do pray for mercy;
And that same prayer doth teach us all to render
The deeds of mercy."*

["It droppeth, as the gentle rain from heaven."]

This splendid idea might have been derived from the 32nd chapter of Deuteronomy, or from the 29th chapter of Job, or from a vague recollection of both passages, where a similar sentiment is to be found.

———— "my doctrine *shall drop as the rain, my speech shall distil as the dew, as the small rain* upon the tender herb, and *as showers* upon the grass."—Deut. xxxii. chap., 2 v.

["It is twice bless'd."]

"Blessed are the merciful: for they shall obtain mercy."—Matthew v. chap., 7 verse.

["It blesseth him that gives, and him that takes."]

"The merciful man doeth good to his own soul."—Prov. xi. chap., 17 verse.

As well as 'blesseth him' upon whom he exercises benignity.

["'Tis mightiest in the mightiest."]

"As his [the Lord's] *majesty* is, so is his *mercy.*"—Ecclesiasticus ii. chap., 18 verse.

THE MERCHANT OF VENICE. 165

[——"it becomes
The *throned monarch* better than his *crown.*"]

" Mercy and truth preserve the king : and his *throne* is upholden by *mercy.*"—Proverbs xx. chap., 28 verse.

Job says, too—

"The blessing of him that *was ready to perish* came upon me :

"I put on *righteousness*, and it clothed me : my *judgment* was as a robe and a *diadem.*"

[" Mercy droppeth as the gentle rain."]

" Unto me men gave ear."

———— " *my speech dropped upon them*, and they waited for me *as for the rain*, &c.

"I chose out their way, and sat chief, and dwelt *as a king in the army*, as *one that comforteth the mourners.*" Job xxix. chap., 13, 14, 21, 22, 23, and 25 verses.

[" It is an attribute to God himself."]

" Blessed be God . . . . the *Father of mercies*, and *God of all comfort.*"—2 Cor. 1 chap., 3 verse.

" His mercy endureth for ever."—cxxxvi. Psalm.

[" Earthly power doth then shew likest God's,
When *mercy seasons justice.*"]

" What doth the Lord require of thee, but to *do justly and to love mercy.*"—Micah vi. chap., 8 verse.

[" In the course of *justice*, none of us *should see salvation.*"]

" Not by works of righteousness *which we have done*,

but *according to his mercy he saved us.*"—Epistle to Titus, iii. chap.

[" *We do pray for mercy;*
And *that same prayer* doth *teach us all to render the deeds of mercy.*"]

An allusion, surely, to that passage in the Lord's prayer—"Forgive us our sins; for we also forgive every one that is indebted to us."—Luke xi. chap., 4 verse.

ACT IV.　SCENE I.

"*Bassanio.* Wrest once the law to your authority:
To do a great right, do a little wrong;
And curb this cruel devil of his will.
　Portia (in the character of a Doctor of laws.) It must
　　not be; there is no power in Venice
Can alter a decree established:
'Twill be recorded for a precedent;
And many an error by the same example,
Will rush into the state: it cannot be.
　Shylock. A Daniel come to judgment! yea, a Daniel!
O wise young judge, how do I honour thee!"

Gratiano says too, when he hears that the Jew must not shed a drop of blood, or take more than a just pound of flesh, otherwise by law he dies, and his goods are confiscate—

" A second Daniel, a Daniel, Jew!
Now, infidel, I have thee on the hip."

Also again—

"A Daniel, still say I; a second Daniel!
I thank thee, Jew, for teaching me that word."

When Portia says—

"He hath refused it (his principal) in the open court;
He shall have merely justice, and his bond."

["A *Daniel* come to *judgment!* O *wise young judge*—a second *Daniel*, a *Daniel*, Jew."—These expressions in praise of Portia, Bassanio's wife, in the habit of a doctor of laws, evidently arose from a knowledge of the history of Susanna. For a young man named Daniel takes as prominent a part there in delivering Susanna from the doom of incontinence—a crime with which, though innocent, she is charged by two elders, as Portia does in protecting Anthonio, her husband's friend, from the malice of Shylock. We will now give extracts of this history from the Apocrypha—

"Therefore when she (Susanna) was led to be put to death, *the Lord raised up the holy spirit of a young youth, whose name was Daniel.*" Hist. Susanna, 45th verse.

"So he, standing in the midst of them (the people), said, Are ye such fools, ye sons of Israel, that, without examination or knowledge of the truth, ye have condemned a daughter of Israel?" 48th verse.

"Return again *to the place of judgment*, for they (the two elders) have borne *false witness against her.*" 49th verse.

Success was soon the result—

"And *Daniel convicted them* of false witness by their own mouth." 61st verse.

"Thus the innocent blood was saved the same day." Part of the 62nd verse.

"And from that day forth was *Daniel had in great reputation* in the sight of the people." Hist. Susanna, 64th verse.

ACT V. SCENE I.

"*Nerissa.* There do I give to you, and Jessica,
From the rich Jew, a special deed of gift,
After his death, of all he dies possess'd of.
   Lorenso. Fair ladies, you *drop manna* in the way of
      starved people."

["Drop manna in the way of starved people."] —This idea is clearly to be traced to the book of Exodus, from which we abstract our proof:—

"And the whole congregation of the children of Israel murmured against Moses and Aaron in the wilderness:

"And the children of Israel said unto them *
            Ye have brought us forth into this wilderness, *to kill this whole assembly with hunger.*

"Then said the Lord unto Moses, Behold, I will *rain bread from heaven* for you; and the people shall go out and gather a certain rate every day, that I may prove them, whether they will walk in my law, or no.

"And it shall come to pass, that on the sixth day they shall prepare that which they bring in; and it shall be twice as much as they gather daily. * * *

"And the Lord spake unto Moses, saying,

"I have heard the murmurings of the children of Israel: speak unto them, saying, At even ye shall eat flesh, and *in the morning ye shall be filled with bread.*

"And it came to pass, that at even the quails came up, and covered the camp; and in the morning the dew lay round about the host.

"And when the dew that lay was gone up, behold, upon the face of the wilderness *there lay a small round thing,* as small as the hoar frost, on the ground.

"And when the children of Israel *saw it, they said* one to another, It is manna." Exod. xvi. 2—15.

CHAPTER XXII.

THE WINTER'S TALE.

ACT I. SCENE II.

Leontes, King of Sicilia, unjustly suspects that his Queen, Hermione, has been dishonoured by Polixenes, King of Bohemia.

"*Camillo.* I am appointed him to murder you.
Polixenes. By whom, Camillo?
Camillo. By the king.
Polixenes. For what?
Camillo. He thinks, nay, with all confidence he
    swears,
As he had seen't, or been an instrument
To vice you to't—that you have touch'd his queen
    forbiddenly.
Polixenes. Oh! then my best blood turn
To an infected jelly; *and my name*
Be yok'd with his, that did betray the best!"

["Be yok'd with his, that did betray the

best!"]—What a strong repudiation of guilt have we, in this allusion to the betrayal of our Lord by Judas Iscariot!

ACT III. SCENE II.

From the defence which Hermione makes in a court of justice, when arraigned there by the jealous Leontes:—

"*Hermione.* You, my lord, best know
(Who least will seem to do so) my past life
Hath been as continent, as chaste, as true,
As I am now unhappy; which is more
Than history can pattern, though devis'd,
And play'd, to take spectators: For behold me,
A fellow of the royal bed, which owe
A moiety of the throne, a great king's daughter,
The mother to a hopeful prince,—here standing,
To prate and talk for life, and honour, 'fore
Who please to come and hear. For life, I prize it
As I weigh grief, which I would spare: *for honour,*
'Tis a derivative from me to mine,
And only that I stand for."

["For honour, 'tis a derivative from me to mine."]—This sentiment, which is probably borrowed from Ecclus. iii. 11, cannot be too often impressed upon the female mind:

"The glory of a man is from the honour of his father; and *a mother in dishonour is a reproach to the children.*"—Steevens.

ACT III.   SCENE III.

The clown says to the shepherd, who has just found the infant Perdita—

"You're a made old man; *if the sins of your youth are forgiven you,* you're well to live. Gold! all gold!"

["If the sins of your youth are forgiven you."] —In the Psalms, from whence this thought comes, the words are—

"Remember not *the sins of my youth.*" Psalm xxv. 7.

ACT V.   SCENE III.

Paulina to Hermione, when she presents to her Perdita, the daughter of Leontes, who was taken from her mother when an infant, exposed in the woods, and brought up by a shepherd :—

"Turn, good lady;
Our Perdita is found.   (*Perdita kneels to Hermione*)
Hermione. You gods, look down,
And *from your sacred vials pour your graces
Upon my daughter's head!*"

In the 5th chapter of Revelation and the 8th verse, the prayers of saints are said to be the contents of golden vials :—

"Having every one of them harps, *and golden vials full of odours, which are the prayers of saints.*"

CHAPTER XXIII.

ALL'S WELL THAT ENDS WELL.

Helena, the daughter of Gerard de Narbon, a famous physician, some time since dead, that she may claim Bertram, Count of Rousillon, for a husband, undertakes to cure the King of France of a fistula, by means of a particular recipe, given her by her father on his deathbed.

"*King.* We thank you, maiden;
But must not be so credulous of cure,
When our most learned doctors leave us; and
The congregated college have concluded,
That labouring art can never answer nature
From her inaidable estate—I say we must not
So stain our judgment, or corrupt our hope,
To prostitute our past-cure malady
To empericks; or to dissever so
Our great self and our credit, to esteem
A senseless help, when help past sense we deem.

Helena. My duty then shall pay me for my pains:
I will no more enforce mine office on you;
Humbly entreating from your royal thoughts
A modest one, to bear me back again.

King. I cannot give thee less, to be call'd grateful:
Thou thought'st to help me; and such thanks I give,
As one near death to those that wish him live:
But, what at full I know, thou know'st no part;
I knowing all my peril, thou no art.

Helena. What I can do, can do no hurt to try,
Since you set up your rest 'gainst remedy:
He that of greatest works is finisher,
Oft does them by the weakest minister:
So holy writ in babes hath judgment shown,
When judges have been babes. Great floods have flown
From simple sources; and *great seas have dry'd,*
When miracles have by the greatest been deny'd.
Oft expectation fails, and most oft there
Where most it promises; and oft it hits,
Where hope is coldest, and despair most sits."

["He that of greatest works is finisher, oft does them by the weakest minister."]—"But God hath chosen the foolish things of the world to confound the wise; and God hath chosen the weak things of the world to confound the things which are mighty." 1 Cor. i. 27.

["So holy writ in babes hath judgment shown, when judges have been babes."]—"And when the chief priests and scribes saw the wonderful things that he did, and the children crying in the temple, and saying, Hosanna to the Son of David; they were sore displeased,

"And said unto him, Hearest thou what these say?
And Jesus saith unto them, Yea; have ye never read,
Out of the mouth of babes and sucklings thou hast
perfected praise?" Matt. xxi. 15, 16.

[" *Great floods have flown* from SIMPLE SOURCES; and
great seas have dry'd."]—" Oh that men would praise
the Lord for his goodness, and for his wonderful works
to the children of men!

" *He turneth rivers into a wilderness,* and the *watersprings into a dry ground.* * * * *

" *He turneth the wilderness into a standing water,* and
DRY GROUND *into watersprings.*" Psalm cvii. 31, 33, 35.

Again, in Psalm cxiv.:—

[" *Great seas have dry'd,* when miracles have by the
greatest been denied."]—" When Israel went out of
Egypt, the house of Jacob from a people of strange
language;

"Judah was his sanctuary, and Israel his dominion.

" *The sea saw it, and fled:* Jordan was driven back.

"Tremble thou earth, at the presence of the Lord, at
the presence of the God of Jacob."

[" Great floods have flown from simple sources."]—
"Which turned *the rock into a standing water,* THE
FLINT *into a fountain of waters.*" Psalm cxiv. 1, 2, 3,
7, 8.

ACT IV. SCENE V.

Lafeu, an old lord, thus speaks of Helena, who
has been deserted by Bertram, Count of Rousillon:

"*Lafeu.* 'Twas a good lady, 'twas a good lady: we may pick a thousand salads, ere we light on such another herb.

Clown. Indeed, sir, she was the sweet-marjoram of the salad, or, rather, the herb of grace.

Lafeu. They are not salad-herbs, you knave, they are nose-herbs.

Clown. I am *no great Nebuchadnezzar,* sir, I have *not much skill in grass.*"

["No great Nebuchadnezzar; I have not much skill in grass."]—An allusion to the punishment inflicted by the Almighty upon this haughty king for his pride:—

"The king spake, and said, Is not this great Babylon, that I have built for the house of the kingdom, by the might of my power, and for the honour of my majesty?

"While the word was in the king's mouth, there fell a voice from heaven, saying, O king Nebuchadnezzar, to thee it is spoken; The kingdom is departed from thee.

"And they shall drive thee from men, and thy dwelling shall be with the beasts of the field: they shall *make thee to eat grass* as oxen, and seven times shall pass over thee, until thou know that the Most High ruleth in the kingdom of men, and giveth it to whomsoever he will.

"The same hour was the thing fulfilled upon Nebuchadnezzar: and he was driven from men, and *did eat grass as oxen,* and his body was wet with the dew of heaven, till his hairs were grown like eagles' feathers, and his nails like birds' claws." Dan. iv. 30–33.

Again—

ACT IV. SCENE V.

CLOWN *to* LAFEU, *an old Lord.*

"*Clown.* Why, sir, if I cannot serve you, I can serve as great a prince as you are.

Lafeu. Who's that? a Frenchman?

Clown. Faith, sir, he has an English name; but his phisnomy is more hotter in France, than there.

Lafeu. What prince is that?

Clown. The black prince, sir; *alias* the prince of darkness; *alias* the devil.

Lafeu. Hold thee, there's my purse: I give thee not this to suggest thee from thy master thou talk'st of; serve him still.

Clown. I am a woodland fellow, sir, that always loved a great fire; and the master I speak of, ever keeps a good fire. *But, sure, he is the prince of the world,* let his nobility remain in his court. *I am for the house with the narrow gate,* which I take to be too little for pomp to enter: some that humble themselves may; but *the many will be* too chill and tender; and they'll be *for the flowery way, that leads to the broad gate, and the great fire.*"

These words of the servant are very tart—show the wide gap that may exist between men of high and low degree, and the feelings that are awakened in the bosom of the latter class, if they think that they are held in contempt by those that sit in high places.

["But, sure, *he is the prince of the world.*"]—From the 14th chapter of St. John. "Peace I leave with you, my peace I give unto you: not as the world giveth, give I unto you.

"Hereafter I will not talk much with you : *for the prince of this world cometh,* and hath nothing in me." John xiv. 27, 30.

["I am for the house with the narrow gate; *but the many, they'll be for the flowery way, that leads to the broad gate, and the great fire.*"]—"*Enter ye in at the strait gate : for wide is the gate, and broad is the way, that leadeth to destruction, and many there be which go in thereat :*

"Because *strait is the gate, and narrow is the way,* which leadeth unto life, and few there be that find it." Matt. vii. 13, 14.

["The many will be too chill and tender; and *they'll be for the flowery way.*"]—These thoughts seem to have sprung from some recollection of passages in the 2nd chapter of the Wisdom of Solomon : the words of the ungodly are there said to be—"Let us enjoy the good things that are present : and let us speedily use the creatures like as in youth.

"Let us fill ourselves with costly wine and ointments: *and let no flower of the spring pass by us.*" ii. 6, 7.

As it is not our intention to investigate any of the plays of Shakespeare which have been pronounced *doubtful,* six more of them, viz., Love's Labour lost; Much Ado About Nothing; As

You Like It; Taming of the Shrew; Measure for Measure; and Comedy of Errors—will complete the list of those which are universally allowed to be emanations of his genius.

CHAPTER XXIV.

THE PLAY OF LOVE'S LABOUR LOST.

The King of Navarre, and the Lords Biron, Dumain, and Longaville, make a vow that no woman shall approach them at the court of Navarre till they have passed three years in deep and painful study. They are soon, however, all forsworn; for the King makes love to the Princess of France, a short time after he and his lords subscribed their names to the schedule touching their oath, and the three lords become suitors to the ladies who attend the princess. Thus Biron sues Rosaline; Longaville, Maria; and Dumain, Katharine. Yet in this play Shakespeare intersperses, besides other biblical examples, several characters that are connected with sacred history. The characters are these—Adam, Eve, Cain, Judas Iscariot, Holofernes, Nathaniel, Judas Maccabeus, Samson, and Solomon.

ACT I.   SCENE II.

DON ADRIANO DE ARMADO, *a fantastical Spaniard, and* MOTH, *his Page.*

"*Armado.* What great men have been in love?
Moth. Hercules, master.
Armado. Most sweet Hercules!—More authority, dear boy, name more; and, sweet my child, let them be men of good repute and carriage.
Moth. Samson, master : he was a man of good carriage, great carriage ; *for he carried the town gates on his back, like a porter:* and he was in love.
Armado. O well-knit Samson! strong-jointed Samson! I do excel thee in my rapier, *as much as thou didst me in carrying gates.* I am in love too—Who was Samson's love, my dear Moth?
Moth. A woman, master.
Armado. Of what complexion?"

["As thou didst me in carrying gates. I am in love too—Who was Samson's love?"]—"Then went Samson to Gaza, and saw there an harlot, and went in unto her.

"And it was told the Gazites, saying, Samson is come hither. And they compassed him in, and laid wait for him all night in the gate of the city, and were quiet all the night, saying, In the morning, when it is day, we shall kill him.

"And Samson lay till midnight, and arose at midnight, *and took the doors of the gate of the city, and the* two *posts, and went away with them, bar and all,* and *put them upon his shoulders,* and carried them up to the top of an hill, that is before Hebron." Jud. xvi. 1—3.

ACT I.   CLOSE OF SCENE II.

"*Armado.* Love is a familiar; love is a devil: there is no evil angel but love. Yet *Samson* was so tempted; and he had excellent strength: yet *was Solomon so seduced;* and he had a very good wit."

["Yet was Solomon so seduced; and he had a very good wit."]—" So king Solomon exceeded all the kings of the earth for riches *and for wisdom.*

"And all the earth sought to Solomon, *to hear his wisdom,* which God had put in his heart." 1 Kings x. 23, 24.

"But King Solomon *loved many strange women,* (together with the daughter of Pharaoh,) women of the Moabites, Ammonites, Edomites, Zidonians, and Hittites;

"Of the nations concerning which the Lord said unto the children of Israel, Ye shall not go in to them, neither shall they come in unto you: for surely they will turn away your heart after their gods: *Solomon clave unto these in love.*

"And he had seven hundred wives, princesses, and three hundred concubines: and his wives turned away his heart.

"For it came to pass, when Solomon was old, that his wives turned away his heart after other gods: and his heart was not perfect with the Lord his God, as was the heart of David his father." 1 Kings xi. 1—4.

ACT III. SCENE I.

"*Biron.* O!—and I, forsooth, in love!
I, that have been love's whip;
A very beadle to a humorous sigh;
A critic; nay, a night-watch constable;
A domineering pedant o'er the boy,
Than whom no mortal so magnificent!
This *wimpled*, whining, purblind, wayward boy."

[" This *wimpled*."]—The *wimple* was a hood or veil which fell over the face.

In Isaiah iii. 22, we find, " The mantles, and the *wimples*, and the crisping-pins."—*Steevens.*

ACT IV. SCENE II.

DULL, *a Constable,* SIR NATHANIEL, *a Curate, and* HOLOFERNES, *a Schoolmaster.*

"*Dull.* You two are book-men; Can you tell by your wit,
What was a month old at *Cain's birth,* that's not five weeks old as yet?"

Shakespeare makes a shrewd hit here. For to this day, how delighted are the unlearned if they can pose their parson or parish schoolmaster (both, perhaps, thought to be powerful in the Scriptures) with some such humorous device as the one just mentioned.

The glory of conquest is great if such a riddle should be unsolved; because either parson or schoolmaster is then beaten on his own ground. Dull, an unlettered man, puts this puzzle relative *to Cain's birth* to Sir Nathaniel, a curate, and Holofernes, a schoolmaster; and with playful malice hopes to baffle them, in spite of their acknowledged superiority as book-men to himself. The replies made to Dull are very characteristic of the persons who make them; each is pedantic in his own way.

"*Dull.* You two are book-men; Can you tell by your wit,
What was a month old at *Cain's birth*, that's not five weeks old as yet?
Holofernes. Dictynna, good man Dull; Dictynna, good man Dull.
Dull. What is Dictynna?
Sir Nathaniel. A title to Phœbe, to Luna, to the moon.
Holofernes. The *moon* was a month old, when *Adam was no more;*
And raught not five weeks, when he came to fivescore.
The allusion holds in the exchange."

Thus is Master Dull driven, contrary to his expectation, from his position; and thus is he worsted by these "book-men," as he calls them.

The schoolmaster, not content with giving the poor constable a perplexing answer, next substitutes, in a triumphant couplet, the word Adam for Cain; and then sums up the case by stating, with the calm dignity of intellectual superiority, that the "*allusion*" (which Dull calls "*collusion*" and "*pollusion*" in assenting to the remark) "holds in the exchange."

The name *Nathaniel* seems to be taken from the 8th chapter, and the name *Holofernes* from the 11th chapter of the Book of Judith. Nathaniel, there written Nathanael, was a forefather of the pious and beautiful Hebrew widow, Judith, who smote Holofernes at his servant's feast, when she was left alone with him in his tent.

["Nathaniel."]—" Now at that time Judith heard thereof, which was the daughter of Merari, the son of Ox, the son of Joseph, the son of Oziel, the son of Elcia, the son of Ananias, the son of Gedeon, the son of Raphaim, the son of Acitho, the son of Eliu, the son of Eliab, *the son of Nathanael*, the son of Samael, the son of Salasadai, the son of Israel." Judith viii. 1.

Holofernes, the chief captain of Nabuchodonosor, king of the Assyrians, intended to enslave the Jews, and to put an end to their religion. He was on this account deceived by Judith, and slain by her, when, "lying along filled with wine," under the canopy of his bed, and then by her decapitated.

[Holofernes."]—In the 11th chapter, Judith

flatters Holofernes, and thus paves the way to his ruin. We will introduce a passage from this chapter, which, with the story to which it belongs, might induce Shakespeare to call the pedant in Love's Labour Lost, Holofernes.

Judith says to Holofernes—

"We have heard of *thy wisdom and thy policies*, and it is reported in all the earth, that thou only art excellent in all the kingdom, *and mighty in knowledge*, and wonderful in feats of war." Judith xi. 8.

ACT IV.   SCENE III.

"*Longaville.* Dumain, thy love is far from charity,
That in love's grief desir'st society : (*Coming forward.*)
You may look pale, but I should blush, I know,
To be o'erheard, and taken napping so.
   King. Come, sir, you blush; as his, your case is
        such ;   (*Coming forward.*)
You chide at him, offending twice as much :
You do not love Maria ; Longaville
Did never sonnet for her sake compile ;
Nor never lay'd his wreathed arms athwart
His loving bosom, to keep down his heart ;
I have been closely shrouded in this bush,
And mark'd you both, and for you both did blush."

The King adds a little further on—

"What will Biron say, when that he shall hear
A faith infringèd, with such zeal did swear?

How will he scorn? how will he spend his wit?
How will he triumph, leap, and laugh at it?
For all the wealth that ever I did see,
I would not have him know so much by me.
   Biron. Now step I forth to whip hypocrisy—
Ah! good my liege, I pray thee pardon me:
                            (*Coming forward.*)
Good heart, what grace hast thou, thus to reprove
These worms for loving, that art most in love?"

The Psalmist says, too—

"I am *a worm and no man.*" Psalm xxii. 6.

See also Job xxv. 6.

" *Your eyes do make no coaches;*
        [*Here* BIRON *alludes to a passage in the*
          KING'S *sonnet to the* PRINCESS.]
            in your tears,
There is no certain princess that appears?
You'll not be perjur'd, 'tis a hateful thing;
Tush, none but minstrels like of sonneting.
But are you not asham'd? nay, are you not,
All three of you, to be thus much o'ershot?
You found his mote; the king your mote did see;
But I a beam do find in each of three.
Oh! what a scene of foolery I have seen,
Of sighs, of groans, of sorrow, and of teen!
O me, with what strict patience have I sat,
To see a king transformed to a gnat!
To see great Hercules whipping a gigg,
And *profound Solomon tuning a jigg.*"

["You found his *mote;* the king your *mote* did see;

But I a *beam* do find in each of three."]—"Judge not, that ye be not judged.

"For with what judgment ye judge, ye shall be judged: and with what measure ye mete, it shall be measured to you again.

"And why beholdest thou *the mote that is in thy brother's eye,* but *considerest not the beam that is in thine own eye?*

"Or how wilt thou say to thy brother, *Let me pull out the mote out of thine eye;* and, behold, *a beam is in thine own eye?*

"Thou hypocrite, first cast out *the beam* out of thine own eye; and then shalt thou see clearly *to cast out the mote* out of thy brother's eye." Matt. vii. 1—5.

["And *profound Solomon tuning a jigg.*"]—This thought may have been taken from a passage in the 3rd chapter of Ecclesiastes—

"There is a time to weep, and a time to laugh; a time to mourn, *and a time to dance.*" Eccles. iii. 4.

Or perhaps from a passage in Ecclesiastes, 2nd chapter—

"I gat me men singers and women singers, *and the delights of the sons of men, as musical instruments, and that of all sorts.*" Eccles. ii. 8.

ACT IV. SCENE III.

In Biron's speech, which begins thus—

" Oh ! 'tis more than need !—
Have at you then, affection's men at arms :
Consider what you first did swear unto ;—
To fast—to study—and to see no woman ;—
Flat treason 'gainst the kingly state of youth."

We find, with one slight omission, the following termination—

" From women's eyes this doctrine I derive :
They sparkle still the right Promethean fire ;
They are the books, the arts, the academes,
That show, contain, and nourish all the world ;
Else none at all in aught proves excellent :
Then fools you were, these women to forswear ;
Or, keeping what is sworn, you will prove fools.
　　　*　　*　　*　　*　　*
Let us once *lose our oaths to find ourselves*,
Or, else we lose ourselves to keep our oaths :
It is religion, to be thus forsworn :
For charity itself fulfils the law ;
And who can sever love from charity ?"

[" Charity itself fulfils the law."]—" Love is the fulfilling of the law." Rom. xiii. 10.

This scene terminates with remarks which may have been suggested by certain parts of the 31st chapter of Job—

"*Biron.* Allons! Allons! *sow'd cockle reaped no corn;*
And justice always whirls in equal measure:
Light wenches may prove plagues to men forsworn;
If so, *our copper buys* no better treasure."

" Sow'd cockle reap'd no corn; justice *always whirls in equal measure.*"]—" If I have walked with vanity, or if my foot hath hasted to deceit;

" Let me *be weighed in an even balance,* that God may know mine integrity.

" If *my step hath turned out of the way, and mine heart walked after mine eyes,* and if any blot hath cleaved to mine hands;

" *Then let me sow, and let another eat;* yea, let my *offspring be rooted out.*" Job xxxi. 5—8.

" If my land cry against me, or that the furrows likewise thereof complain;

" If I have eaten the fruits thereof *without money,* or *have caused the owners thereof* to lose their life:

" Let thistles grow instead of wheat, *and cockle instead of barley.*" Job xxxi. 38—40.

ACT V. SCENE I.

DON ADRIANO DE ARMADO, *and* HOLOFERNES, *a Schoolmaster, also* NATHANIEL, *the Curate.*

" *Armado.* The very all of all is—but, sweetheart, I do implore secresy—that the king would have me present the princess, sweet chuck, with some delightful ostentation, or show, or pageant, or antic, or fire-work. Now, understanding that the curate, and your sweet self, are good at such eruptions, and sudden breakings out of mirth, as it were, I have acquainted you withal, to the end to crave your assistance.

Holofernes. Sir, you shall present before her the nine worthies.—Sir Nathaniel, as concerning some entertainment of time, some show in the posterior of this day, to be rendered by our assistance—at the king's command; and this most gallant, illustrate, and learned gentleman—before the princess; I say, none so fit as to present the nine worthies.

Nathaniel. Where will you find men worthy enough to present them?

Holofernes. Joshua, yourself; myself, or this gallant gentleman, *Judas Maccabæus.*"

["Joshua, yourself; myself, *Judas Maccabæus.*"] For these names see 1st Book of Maccabees, 2nd chapter.

"Jesus [*i. e.,* Joshua] for fulfilling the word, was made a judge in Israel." 1 Mac. ii. 55.

"As for *Judas Maccabeus,* he hath been mighty and strong, even from his youth up: let him be your captain, and fight the battle of the people." 1 Mac. ii. 66.

This Judas, surnamed Maccabæus, one of the Asmoneans, by bravery and skill vanquished the Syrians, cleared the temple of heathen profanation, and restored to the Jews their ancient religion.

ACT V. SCENE II.

"*King.* Farewell, mad wenches; you have simple wits.

Exeunt KING *and his Lords,* BIRON, LONGAVILLE, *and* DUMAIN, *disguised like Muscovites.*

"*Princess.* Twenty adieus, my frozen Muscovites. Are these the breed of wits so wonder'd at?
Boyet. Tapers they are, with your sweet breaths puff'd out.
Rosaline. Well-liking wits they have; gross, gross; fat, fat."

["Well-liking wits."]—Well-liking is the same as *embonpoint.* So in Job xxxix. 4.

"Their young ones are *in good liking.*"—Steevens.

ACT V. SCENE II.

Where the KING, BIRON, LONGAVILLE, *and* DUMAIN, *enter in their own habits.*

"*King.* Fair sir———Where is the princess?
Boyet. Gone to her tent: Please it your majesty, Command me any service to her?
King. That she vouchsafe me audience for one word.
Boyet. I will; and so will she, I know, my lord."
(*Exit.*)

Biron says of Boyet, amongst other remarks which he now makes upon him—

"This gallant pins the wenches on his sleeve;
Had he been Adam, he had tempted Eve:"

in his speech which terminates with the couplet—

"And consciences, that will not die in debt,
Pay him the due of honey-tongued Boyet."

["Had he been Adam he had tempted Eve."]— A sly bit of humour, and fantastic transposition of the historical fact, alluded to by Adam in the 12th verse of the 3rd chapter of Genesis—

"And the man said, The woman whom thou gavest to be with me, she gave me of the tree, and I did eat."

Again—

ACT V. SCENE II.

"*King.* Here is like to be a good presence of worthies: He presents Hector of Troy; the swain, Pompey the Great; the parish curate, Alexander; Armado's page, Hercules; the pedant, *Judas Maccabæus.*

Enter HOLOFERNES *for* JUDAS.

Holofernes. Judas I am——
Dumain. A Judas!
Holofornes. Not Iscariot, sir.
Judas I am, ycleped Maccabæus.
Dumain. Judas Maccabæus clipt, is plain Judas.
Biron. A kissing traitor:—How art thou prov'd
   Judas?
Holofernes. Judas I am——

Dumain. The more shame for you, Judas.
Holofernes. What mean you, sir?
Boyet. To make Judas hang himself.
Holofernes. Begin, sir; you are my elder.
Biron. Well follow'd: Judas was hang'd on an elder."

[" *Dumain.* A Judas! *Holofernes.* Not Iscariot, sir."]—Shakespeare evidently remembers the words relative to Judas, the brother of James, in the 22nd verse of the 14th chap. of St. John—

" Judas saith unto him, not Iscariot."

[" *Judas* I am, ycleped Maccabæus. Judas Maccabæus clipt, is plain *Judas.*"]—*Judas,* for *Judas Maccabæus,* occurs several times in the 1st Book of Maccabees, chapter iii.

". Then his (Mattathias) son *Judas,* called Maccabeus, rose up in his stead." 1 Mac. iii. 1.

" Apollonius gathered the Gentiles together, and a great host out of Samaria, to fight against Israel.

" Which thing, when *Judas* perceived, he went forth to meet him, and so he smote him, and slew him: many also fell down slain, but the rest fled.

" Wherefore *Judas* took their spoils, and Apollonius' sword also, and therewith he fought all his life long." 1 Mac. iii. 10—12.

" Then began the fear of *Judas* and his brethren, and an exceeding great dread, to fall upon the nations round about them: Insomuch as his fame came unto the king, and all nations talked of the battles of *Judas.*" 1 Mac. iii. 25, 26.

"And *Judas* said, Arm yourselves, and be valiant men, and see that ye be in readiness against the morning, that ye may fight with these nations that are assembled together against us, to destroy us and our sanctuary." 1 Mac. iii. 58.

["A kissing traitor: How art thou prov'd *Judas?* *Judas I am.* The more shame for you, *Judas.*"]— "Then one of the twelve, called *Judas Iscariot*, went unto the chief priests,

"And said unto them, What will ye give me, and I will deliver him unto you? And they covenanted with him for thirty pieces of silver." Matt. xxvi. 14, 15.

"Now he that betrayed him gave them a sign, saying. *Whomsoever I shall kiss*, that same is he: hold him fast." Matt. xxvi. 48.

["A kissing traitor."]—Judas is called *traitor* in Luke vi. 16—

"And *Judas Iscariot*, which also was the *traitor*."

["What mean you, sir? To make *Judas hang himself.*"]—"Then Judas, which had betrayed him, when he saw that he was condemned, repented himself, and brought again the thirty pieces of silver to the chief priests and elders,

"Saying, I have sinned, in that I have betrayed the innocent blood. And they said, What is that to us? See thou to that.

"And he cast down the pieces of silver in the temple, and departed, and *went and hanged himself.*" Matt. xxvii. 3—5.

CHAPTER XXIV.

MUCH ADO ABOUT NOTHING.

LEONATO, *Governor of Messina, and* BEATRICE *his Niece.*

"*Leonato.* Well, niece, I hope to see you one day fitted with a husband.

Beatrice. Not till God make men of some other metal than earth. Would it not grieve a woman to be *over-master'd with a piece of valiant dust?* to make an account of her life to a clod of wayward marl? No, uncle; I'll none: *Adam's sons are my brethren,* and truly, I hold it *a sin to match in my kindred.*"

It is evident to what parts of Holy Writ this humorous speech has reference.

[" To be over-master'd with a piece of valiant dust."] —" In the sweat of thy face shalt thou eat bread, till thou return *unto the ground; for out of it wast thou taken: for dust thou art,* and unto dust shalt thou return."

["Adam's sons are my brethren."]—"And Adam called his wife's name Eve; because she was *the mother of all living.*" Gen. iii. 19, 20.

["A sin to match in my kindred."]—"None of you shall approach *to any that is near of kin* to him." Lev. xviii. 6.

ACT II. SCENE I.

"*Don Pedro.* Now, signior, where's the count? Did you see him?

Benedick. Troth, my lord, I have played the part of lady Fame. I found him here *as melancholy as a lodge in a warren.*"

["Lodge in a warren."]—A parallel thought occurs in the first chapter of Isaiah, where the prophet, describing the desolation of Judah, says—

"The daughter of Zion *is left as a cottage in a vineyard, as a lodge in a garden of cucumbers.*"—Steevens.

ACT I. SCENE II.

DON PEDRO *and* BENEDICK.

"*Don Pedro.* The lady Beatrice hath a quarrel to you; the gentleman that danced with her, told her, that she is much wronged by you.

Benedick. Oh! she misused me past the endurance of a block; an oak, but with one green leaf on it, would have answered her; my very visor began to assume life, and scold with her: she told me, not thinking I had been myself, that I was the prince's jester; that I was duller than a great thaw; huddling jest upon jest, with such impossible conveyance, upon me, that I stood like a man at a mark, with a whole army shooting at me: she speaks poniards, and every word stabs: if her breath were as terrible as her terminations, there were no living near her, she would infect to the north star. *I would not marry her, though she were endow'd with all that Adam had left him before he transgress'd."*

[* * * "that Adam had left him before he transgress'd."]—This assertion owes its pungency to the effect it has upon our imagination; for it really means, no wealth that she *might* possess would induce me to marry her.

"O Lord, who bearest rule, thou spakest at the beginning, when thou didst plant the earth, and that thyself alone. * * *

"And gavest *a body unto Adam* without soul, which was the workmanship of thine hands, and didst breathe into him the breath of life, and he was made living before thee.

"And thou *leddest him into paradise, which thy right hand had planted,* before ever the earth came forward.

"And unto him thou gavest commandment to love thy way: which he transgressed." * * * *
2 Esdras iii. 4—7.

ACT III. SCENE III.

"*Borachio.*———Thou knowest, that the fashion of a doublet, or a hat, or a cloak, is nothing to a man.

Conrade. Yes, it is apparel.

Borachio. I mean, the fashion.

Conrade. Yes, the fashion is the fashion.

Borachio. Tush! I may as well say, the fool's the fool. But see'st thou not, what a deformed thief this fashion is?

Watch. I know that Deformed; he has been a vile thief these seven years; he goes up and down like a gentleman: I remember his name.

Borachio. Didst thou not hear somebody?

Conrade. No; 'twas the vane on the house.

Borachio. See'st thou not, I say, what a deformed thief this fashion is? how giddily he turns about all the hot bloods, between fourteen and five-and-thirty? sometime fashioning them *like Pharaoh's soldiers in the reechy painting;* sometime, *like god Bel's priests in the old church window.*"

Borachio thus ridicules the fashions of his day. The fear lest he should be overheard when speaking of such matters to his friend, is laughably true to nature. His sarcasm is also very natural. A man in his vein might advert to the primitive garbs in the painting, and the odd vestments on the church window; for such subjects as Pharaoh's soldiers, and god Bel's priests, would probably be felt, being sacred, to give zest to the raillery.

The 14th chapter of Exodus might be supposed to supply the subject of the picture.

"And the Lord hardened the heart of Pharaoh king of Egypt, and he pursued after the children of Israel: and the children of Israel went out with an high hand.

"But the Egyptians pursued after them, (all the horses and chariots of Pharaoh, and his horsemen, and his army.") Exod. xiv. 8, 9.

["God Bel's priests."]—Might be representations taken from the story of Bel and the Dragon.

We produce from As You Like It the following apposite evidence—

ACT II.   SCENE I.

The Forest of Arden.
Enter the DUKE *senior, and several* LORDS.

"*Duke senior.* Now, my co-mates, and brothers in exile,
Hath not old custom made this life more sweet
Than that of painted pomp? Are not these woods
More free from peril than the envious court?
Here feel we *but the penalty of Adam,*
The season's difference."

["Here feel we but the penalty of Adam, the season's difference."]—In these woods, where we escape the envy of mankind, our ills are limited to unpleasing effects of weather, the penalty of Adam, when the fall brought a curse upon the earth, and rendered him amenable to the sentence—

"Thou shalt surely die." Gen. ii. 17.

ACT II. SCENE III.

ADAM *and* ORLANDO.

What Christian magnanimity adorns the character of Adam! To give the speech of old Adam its due weight, the words of Orlando, his young master, are here inserted—

"*Orlando.* What, wouldst thou have me go and beg
    my food?
Or, with a base and boisterous sword, enforce
A thievish living on the common road?
This I must do, or know not what to do:
Yet this I will not do, do how I can;
I rather will subject me to the malice
Of a diverted blood, and bloody brother.
  Adam. But do not so: I have five hundred crowns,
The thrifty hire I sav'd under your father,
Which I did store to be my foster-nurse,
When service should in my old limbs lie lame,
And unregarded age in corners thrown;
Take that: and *He that doth the ravens feed,*
Yea, *providently caters for the sparrow,*
Be comfort to my age!"

["He that doth the ravens feed."]—"Consider the ravens: for they neither sow nor reap; which neither have storehouse nor barn; and God feedeth them:

How much more are ye better than the fowls?" Luke xii. 24.

["Yea providently caters for the sparrow."]—"Are not five sparrows sold for two farthings, and not one of them is forgotten before God? But even the very hairs of your head are all numbered. Fear not, therefore: ye are of more value than many sparrows." Luke xii. 6, 7.

CHAPTER XXV.

THE TAMING OF THE SHREW.

ACT V. SCENE II.

"*Kate, the Shrew.* A woman mov'd is like *a fountain troubled,*
Muddy, ill-seeming, thick, bereft of beauty;
And, while it is so, *none so dry or thirsty
Will deign to sip, or touch one drop of it.*"

In this extract from the lecture of the shrew, on the duties of wives towards their husbands, and in the 5th chapter of Proverbs, the word *fountain* denotes a *wife*—

E. G., "Let thy *fountain* be blessed : and rejoice with *the wife* of thy youth." Prov. v. 18.

But nowhere in the Proverbs does "*a fountain troubled*" denote a shrew. Shakespeare, it seems, met with the words *a troubled fountain* in the 25th chapter of Proverbs—

E. G., "A righteous man falling down before the wicked is as *a troubled fountain*, and a corrupt spring"—

transferred them from thence into the play, and affixed to them their present meaning.

A like metaphorical way of speaking to this, "*None so dry or thirsty, will deign to sip or touch one drop of it*," is to be found in the 5th chapter of Proverbs—

E. G., "Drink waters out of thine own cistern." Prov. v. 15.

We may now place before the reader the results obtained from an investigation of—

CHAPTER XXVI.

MEASURE FOR MEASURE.

ACT I. SCENE II.

The Street.
Enter Lucio *and two Gentlemen.*

"*Lucio.* If the duke, with the other dukes, come not to composition with the king of Hungary, why, then all the dukes fall upon the king.

1 *Gent.* Heaven grant us its peace, but not the king of Hungary's!

2 *Gent.* Amen.

Lucio. Thou concludest like the sanctimonious pirate, that went to sea with the *ten commandments,* but scraped one out of the table.

2 *Gent. Thou shalt not steal?* (See Exod. xx. 15.)

Lucio. Ay, that he raz'd."

ACT I.— SCENE III.

Enter PROVOST, CLAUDIO.

"*Claudio.* Fellow, why dost thou shew me thus to the world?
Bear me to prison, where I am committed.
Provost. I do it not in evil disposition,
But from Lord Angelo by special charge.
Claudio. Thus can the demigod, authority,
Make us pay down for our offence by weight.
The words of heaven;—*on whom it will, it will;
On whom it will not, so; yet still 'tis just.*"

["On whom it will, it will; on whom it will not, so; yet still 'tis just."]—Shakespeare evidently derives this passage from the 9th chapter of St. Paul's epistle to the Romans—

"What shall we say then? Is there unrighteousness with God? God forbid.

"For he saith to Moses, *I will have mercy on whom I will have mercy,* and I will have compassion on whom I will have compassion.

"So then it is not of him that willeth, nor of him that runneth, but of God that showeth mercy.

"For the scripture saith unto Pharaoh, Even for this same purpose have I raised thee up, that I might show my power in thee, and that my name might be declared throughout all the earth.

"Therefore *hath he mercy on whom he will have*

mercy, and whom he will he hardeneth." Rom. ix. 14—18.

ACT II. SCENE II.

ANGELO, *Lord Deputy in the absence of* VINCENTIO, *Duke of Vienna;* ISABELLA, *Sister to* CLAUDIO; *and* LUCIO.

ANGELLO'S *house.*

"*Angelo.* Pray you, begone.
Isabella. I would to Heaven I had your potency,
And you were Isabel! should it then be thus?
No; I would tell what 'twere to be a judge,
And what a prisoner.
Lucio. Ay, touch him: there's the vein. (*Aside.*)
Angelo. Your brother is a forfeit of the law,
And you but waste your words.
Isabella. Alas! alas!
Why, all the souls that were, were forfeit once;
And He that might the vantage best have took,
Found out the remedy: How would you be,
If He, which is the top of judgment, should
But judge you, as you are? Oh! think on that,
And mercy then will breathe within your lips,
Like man new made."

The substance of this passage—

"Why, all the souls that were, were forfeit once;
And He that might the vantage best have took,
Found out the remedy"—

is contained in the 9th chapter of St. Paul's epistle to the Hebrews, the 27th and 28th verses.

"As it is appointed unto men once to die, but after this the judgment:

"So Christ was once offered to bear the sins of many; and unto them that look for him shall he appear the second time without sin unto salvation."

And of this—

"How would you be,
If He, which is the top of judgment, should
But judge you as you are?"

in the 3rd and 4th verses of the 130th Psalm—

"If thou, Lord, shoulds't mark iniquities, O Lord, who shall stand?

"But there is forgiveness with thee, that thou mayest be feared."

"Oh! think on that,
And mercy then will breathe within your lips,
Like man new made."

"*Put on the new man*, which after God is created in righteousness and true holiness.

"And be ye *kind one to another, tender-hearted,* forgiving one another, even as God for Christ's sake hath forgiven you." Eph. iv. 24, 32.

ACT II. SCENE IV.

"*Angelo.*   Redeem thy brother
By yielding up thy body to my will;
Or else he must not only *die the death.*"

We find this expression in Act I. of Midsummer Night's Dream—

"*Theseus.* Either to *die the death,* or to abjure
For ever the society of men."

["Die the death."]—"It is," says Steevens, "a phrase taken from Scripture." We here quote passages in which it is found—

"Whoso curseth father or mother, let him *die the death.*" Mark vii. 10.

Also—

"All flesh waxeth old as a garment: for the covenant from the beginning is, Thou shalt *die the death.*" Ecclus. xiv. 17.

END OF ACT III. SCENE II.

To this short metre couplet—

"He, who the sword of Heav'n will bear,
Should be as holy as severe"—

there is a parallel in the 2nd Book of Samuel, xxiii. 3—

"The God of Israel said, the Rock of Israel spake to me, *He that ruleth over men must be just, ruling in the fear of God.*"

CHAPTER XXVII.

THE COMEDY OF ERRORS

supplies us with more evidence than might, perhaps, be expected from the nature of the subject.

ACT II. SCENE II.

ANTIPHOLIS *of Syracuse, and* DROMIO *of Syracuse.*

"*Antipholis.* Well, sir, *learn to jest in good time; There's a time for all things.*"

Parallel thoughts are expressed in the 3rd chapter of Ecclesiastes—

"*To every thing there is a season,* and a time to every purpose under the heaven." Eccles. iii. 1.

"A time to weep, *and a time to laugh.*" Eccles. iii. 4, (part of it.)

ACT IV. SCENE III.

DROMIO *of Syracuse mistakes the twin* ANTIPHOLIS *for* ANTIPHOLIS *of Ephesus, who was arrested.*

" *Dromio of Syracuse.* Master, here's the gold you sent me for: What, have you got *the picture of old Adam new apparell'd?*

Antip. of Syracuse. What gold is this? What Adam dost thou mean?

Dromio of Syracuse. Not that Adam, that kept the paradise, but that Adam, that keeps the prison: he that goes *in the calf's-skin that was kill'd for the prodigal;* he that came behind you, sir, like an evil angel, and bid you forsake your liberty.

Antip. of Syracuse. I understand thee not."

[" The picture of old Adam new apparell'd."]— The allusion, says Theobald, is to Adam in his state of innocence going naked; and immediately after the fall, being clothed in a frock of skins. Thus he was new apparell'd—

["Not that Adam that kept the paradise."]—It is stated in the 15th verse of the 2nd chapter of Genesis, that Adam was placed in "the garden of Eden to dress it and *to keep it.*"

The word *paradise* is several times to be found in the Apocrypha, *e. g.*, the 2nd Book of Esdras, but not in the Old Testament.

In the 3rd chapter and 6th verse of 2nd Book of Esdras—

"Thou leddest him *into paradise, which thy right hand had planted.*"

Again, in the 6th chapter and 2nd verse of 2nd Book of Esdras—

"Before it thundered and lightened, *or ever the foundations of paradise were laid.*"

Also, in the 7th chapter and 53rd verse of 2nd Book of Esdras—

"And that there should be shewed *a paradise, whose fruit endureth for ever.*"

["He that goes in the calf's-skin that was kill'd for the prodigal."]—In the parable of the Prodigal Son, it is stated that the father of the prodigal said to his servants—

"Bring hither the fatted calf, and kill it; and let us eat, and be merry: For this my son was dead, and is alive again; he was lost, and is found." Luke xv. 23, 24.

ACT IV. SCENE III.

Enter a COURTESAN.

"*Dromio of Syracuse.* Master, is this mistress Satan? *Antip. of Syracuse.* It is the devil."

Dromio of Syracuse, amongst other remarks, says of such characters—"*It is written, They appear to men like angels of light.*"

["Like angels of light."]—There is a sentence very similar to this in the 2nd epistle to the Corinthians, the 11th chapter and 14th verse—

"Satan himself is transformed into an angel of light."

ACT IV. SCENE IV.

PINCH, *a Conjurer, and* ANTIPHOLIS, *of Ephesus.*

"*Pinch.* Give me your hand, and let me feel your pulse.
Antip. There is my hand, and let it feel your ear.
Pinch. I charge thee, Satan, hous'd within this man,
To yield possession to my holy prayers."

["Satan, *hous'd within this man.*"]—"*I will return into my house, from whence I came out,*" says the unclean spirit in Matt. xii. 44, when he seeketh rest in dry places, after his departure out of a man, "but findeth none."

ACT IV. SCENE IV.

"*Pinch.* Mistress, both man and master *is possess'd;*
I know it by their pale and deadly looks:
They *must be bound,* and laid in some dark room."

Again—

"*Pinch.* More company;—the fiend is strong within him."

It seems likely that the miracle wrought, when the devil was ejected from a man and sent into a herd of swine, recurred to the mind of Shakespeare at the time he wrote these lines. The sufferer is said, in the 5th chapter of Mark, *to be possess'd* (the word used in the play) with the devil; he is said to inhabit the tombs, and to be so fierce " that no *man could bind* him."

Having done with strictly parallel passages, it remains to notice resemblances of a general character. The stories of Jacob and Esau—of Joseph and his brethren—many passages in the life of David—and the parable of the Prodigal Son—portray those passions and affections, emphatically styled in Scripture " yearnings of the bowels," much after the manner in which Shakespeare is found to exhibit them. They belong alike to every age and every nation. The very images of Scripture are sometimes the images of Shakespeare. Nothing is more common in the former than the comparison of *good* to light, and *evil* to darkness. Bad men hate the *light* lest their *evil deeds should be reproved.* How tremendously is this feeling displayed by Lady Macbeth!—

" Come, thick night,
And pall thee in the dunnest smoke of hell!
That my keen knife see not the wound it makes;
Nor Heav'n peep through the blanket of the dark,
To cry, Hold, hold!"

Light to Shakespeare suggests the idea of goodness —

"How far that little candle throws his beams!
So shines a good deed in a naughty world."

This is the scriptural, not the common comparison; the latter likens darkness to *sorrow*, and light to *joy*.

Mr. Ruskin notices, in the 4th volume of his "Modern Painters," page 382, that "Shakespeare almost always implies a total difference in *nature* between one human being and another; one being from the birth pure and affectionate, another base and cruel; and he displays each in its sphere as having the nature of the *dove*, *wolf*, or *lion*, never much implying the government or change of nature by any external principle." It is very remarkable that scripture, which teaches us more by *things* than by words, though it recognizes a change of disposition through force of an external principle, does yet not only paint men as of different natures, but describes those natures under the forms of different kinds of animals. Thus the good and the bad are generally typified by the figure of "sheep" and of "goats." Our Saviour calls the Pharisees a "generation of *vipers*." He himself is described as the "LAMB of God." The natures of the heathen about to be converted to the gospel, are described by the prophet as those of wild beasts. "The *wolf* shall dwell with the *lamb*, and the *leopard* shall lie down with the *kid*, and the *calf* and the young *lion*, and the *fatling* together," &c. &c. The kindly affections and inherent purity of Shakespeare's best women, have their type in the character of Ruth. The difference between Ruth and Orpah was simply a difference in degree of dutiful affection.

"Orpah kissed her mother-in-law, but Ruth clave unto her," passionately beseeching leave to follow her fortunes, in the sweetest words which the power of language could supply. But there are parallels of individual character. Lady Macbeth, for instance, the most terrible of Shakespeare's heroines, has her perfect counterpart in Jezebel. The very mind and being of the latter seem to be infused into, and to animate, the former. Holinshed's details of Scottish history connected with this play, do not render these ideas untenable. The same may be said with respect to Ahab and Macbeth till the death of Duncan: the latter then resembles Saul, delivered up to the spirit of evil.

Ahab had his "compunctious visitings," and short-lived repentance; Macbeth his "milk of human kindness," and his religious awe; so that— "what he would highly, that would he holily." Ahab, *whom his wife stirred up*, and Macbeth, seem both, while desiring the *fruits*, similarly to shrink from the *perpetration*, of cold-blooded murder. Hence the former was content to be used as a tool in the murder of Naboth, and the latter became little more than an instrument in that of the King.

It was Jezebel who bestowed upon Ahab the vineyard, as it was Lady Macbeth who gave her husband the kingdom. Both these women began by taunting their husbands into acquiescence with their measures, but both resolve to act for themselves.

Hear Jezebel—"Dost thou now govern the kingdom of Israel? Arise and eat bread, and let thy heart be merry; *I will give thee the vineyard of Naboth, the Jezreelite.*" Lady Macbeth, when informed by letter of the predestined throne, is at first ready to put an end to Duncan herself, a purpose from which she was diverted by his resemblance to her "*father, as he slept.*"

"*Lady Macbeth.*   He that's coming
Must be provided for, and you shall put
This night's great business into *my* despatch.
                [*Here Macbeth betrays irresolution.*
Macbeth. We will speak further.
Lady M. Only look up clear ;
To alter favour, ever, is to fear—
Leave all the rest to me."

Thus Jezebel and Lady Macbeth went on spurring their husbands in their guilty career, till the two latter expiated their crimes upon the field of battle; whilst they themselves came to an equally untimely end. But Macbeth resembles Saul when reprobate, after the murder of the ill-starred Duncan. Thus Macbeth laments that the issue of the slaughtered Banquo must ascend his throne; Saul, that "the kingdom has been rent out of his hand," and given to David (whom he has repeatedly endeavoured to slay) and his descendants. When the witch of Endor had called up Samuel, she exclaimed—"*I saw gods ascending out of the earth!*" Samuel was, however, the only ghost. Now it is evident *that the spirits of Banquo's line, &c.*, could not have been ghosts in the common acceptation of the term, but mere typical shadows; there is, in fact, no ghost but Banquo's throughout the play: a circumstance which did not escape the penetration of Mrs. Montague.* Saul saw, it seems, only Samuel; but he heard the witch's remark, "I saw gods ascending out of the earth"— and Samuel's rebuke, "Why hast thou disquieted me, to bring me up?" he heard, too, the very *words again* which Samuel, when a prophet of the Lord, had addressed to him—and, though he was "*sore afraid because of these words,*" yet so hardened had he become, that he could even be induced to partake of food which the witch of Endor had prepared for him. This demonstration of depravity satisfies us that Macbeth's character, when at its worst stage, is not *untrue* to nature. Hence the effect, both physically and mentally, of witchcraft upon Macbeth, constrains our very *feelings* to a tacit acknowledgment of its truthfulness. More-

* *Vide* Essay on Genius of Shakespeare.

over, the apparitions that were *seen*, and the words that were *heard* by Macbeth—(the prediction relative to Banquo's issue *twice*)—were not more terrific or overwhelming than the things which were revealed to the eyes and ears of Saul.

Let us now direct our attention to Hamlet's conduct after he had received instructions from the ghost of his father: a quotation from scripture shall be produced to account for it. The deaths of Polonius and the King may be said to be accidental effects; Hamlet having been roused to the committal of them, by circumstances which hurried him *from* the motive that *should have led* to the King's death. Hamlet speaks of being "prompted to his revenge by heaven and hell:" by heaven, which considered life forfeited by him who had committed murder, and had merely fixed on Hamlet as the person who should execute this righteous doom: by hell, inasmuch as Hamlet's worst feelings urged him to commit the act. The futility of a lesson from the tomb is here shown; as if the words—"If they hear not Moses and the prophets, neither will they be persuaded though one rose from the dead," were the *source* from whence Shakespeare derived *hints* in this case: for Hamlet's conduct *after* the interview with his father was such as might be expected, especially of one who could say—"We defy augury; there is a special providence in the fall of a sparrow," (see Act V.) he endeavours to find out what this vision might mean. Perplexed at first by doubts and scruples as to what he ought to believe or to do, because "the spirit which he had seen might be the devil," who had perhaps assumed a pleasing shape, taking advantage of Hamlet's weakness and his melancholy (for Hamlet was not *before*, nor had he become, *since* the interview with the ghost, a *religious* man), in order to damn him. He, therefore, determines to have "some players play something like the murder of his father," before the King "his uncle," that he may *prove* the veracity of the story alleged by the ghost. The plot succeeds, and Hamlet has only to strike the blow of vengeance—as Samuel did when he slew Agag—in obedience to the will of Heaven. He seems, however, by this time, from the effects of grief, doubt, and contemplation, *incapable* of taking the vengeance required, though clearly prompted to do so by one "who rose from the dead." The course taken by Hamlet to satisfy himself concerning the ghost, is probably quite original. Thus he first establishes the credibility of the ghost with regard to *real existence*, by the information which he gains from *others* respecting it: he then establishes the credibility of the ghost with regard to *words*, by means of scenic representations. And so anxious is he *then* to arrive at right conclusions respecting his uncle, that he particularly requests Horatio, the man on whose integrity and judgment he can best rely, to watch the king narrowly when *that scene* of the play, which comes near the circumstance of his father's death, is brought before them :—

> "I pr'ythee, when thou see'st that act a-foot,
> Even with the very comment of thy soul
> Observe my uncle : if his occulted guilt
> Do not itself unkennel in one speech,
> It is a *damned* ghost that *we* have seen ;
> And my imaginations are as foul
> As Vulcan's stithy : Give him heedful note :
> For I mine eyes will rivet to his face ;
> And after, *we will both our judgments join*
> In censure of his seeming."

What *should* have been the result, when both their judgments *did* join in censure of his seeming? Why, Hamlet should have killed the king, *because* that king was a usurper and a murderer, in obedience to the ghost's commands. Had the ghost's account of the torments which he suffered, in consequence of having been "cut off in the blossoms of his sin, and sent to his account with all his imperfections on his head," really brought conviction home to Hamlet, and led him to eschew wickedness, since any man *may* be so cut off and sent to his account, he would have inflicted punishment upon his uncle in a right spirit, have satisfied the world of his uncle's guilt, and have made a pious and good king.

But men are not to be persuaded by those who *rise from the dead.* Hamlet, therefore, must not be persuaded by such supernatural agency.

Now, it is *clear* that the parable of Dives and Lazarus had made particular impression on Shakespeare's mind, for it is mentioned several times in the play of Henry IV. by the *same* character; and, as *hints* are sufficient for genius of a high order, it is *probable* that the parable above noticed aided him in this case.

But it may be said, such genius as Shakespeare's would want no aid to enable it either to place the characters of Hamlet and Macbeth in the circumstances which have been already scanned, or to make their subsequent conduct spring so naturally from them. Yet the circumstances in which these men are placed, and the conduct which so naturally results from them (if the sources from whence his ideas are said to flow be not correct), seem as likely to be fictions of *unaided* genius as a statue, *perfectly correct* in its detail, and *gracefully* natural in its attitude, could be thought to be produced by one who was both ignorant of anatomy and the rules of correct taste.

"Shakespeare," says Mr. Ruskin, at the place before quoted—" Shakespeare always leans on the force of fate, as it urges the final evil; and dwells with infinite bitterness on the power of the wicked, and the infinitude of results dependent seemingly on little things. A fool brings the last piece of news from Verona, and the dearest lives of its noble houses are lost; they might have been saved if the sacristan had not stumbled as he walked. Othello mislays his handkerchief, and there remains nothing for him but death. Hamlet gets hold of the wrong foil, and the rest is silence. Edmund's runner is a moment too late at the prison, and the feather will not move at Cordelia's lips. Salisbury a moment too late at the Tower, and Arthur lies on the stones dead. Goneril and Iago have on the whole, in this world, Shakespeare sees, much of their own way, though they come to a bad end. It is a pin that Death pierces the king's fortress wall with; and carelessness and folly sit, sceptred and dreadful, side by side, with the pin-armed skeleton."

If it be thus in Shakespeare, and in the world, it is assuredly the same in the Bible. Jezebel and Judas have it all their own way, though they come to a bad end. In that sacred book, from beginning to end, good men lament that the wicked "flourish" here, "like a green bay-tree." That "they come not into peril like other folk, neither are in trouble like other men." To witness this was the sorest trial of "the man after God's own heart;'' and has been one of the severest trials of the faithful in all ages of the Church. David could not understand this till he "went into the house of God," and understood "the END of these men." Granting a superintending providence, which Shakespeare ever recognizes, things come to pass in the Bible, and in the world, as *by chance.* "The lot is cast into the lap, but the disposal is with the Lord."

The most solemn predictions in Scripture, be it remembered, are fulfilled seemingly by *accident*. In the Bible, if any where, we might be led to expect the gradual development of a plot or principle; whereas we meet with the very reverse of this. It was foretold that Ahab should not return in peace. He accordingly perishes in battle. But how does he perish? The command of the king of Syria to the captains of his chariots, to "fight neither with small nor great, but only with the king of Israel," seems at first sight ordained by God himself for the fulfilment of prophecy. We should therefore expect that Jehoshaphat, to secure his own safety, would have somehow betrayed the disguise of Ahab, that the death of the latter might appear to proceed from *design*. Such, however, was not the case. "A certain man draws a bow *at a venture*, and pierces the king between the joints of his harness." It was also predicted that "dogs should lick his blood." How is this prophecy fulfilled? Is the body exposed to purposed indignity? No, it was *buried*, we have reason to believe, with respect. But "one washed the chariot in the pool of Samaria;" and then the "*dogs* came and licked up the blood," in the usual course of events.

Jehu, indeed, affected to fulfil the prediction concerning Joram, by casting his body into the plot of Naboth, the Jezreelite. But Jehu forgot, and would have left unfulfilled, what had been foretold in the case of Jezebel. He gave orders to *bury* this "cursed woman," because "she was a king's daughter." But he first went in to eat and drink. Before he had finished *his* meal, the dogs had had *theirs;* and then he remembered the word which the Lord had spoken by the mouth of Elijah the Tishbite.

Since, then, what we call *accident* seems to be the ruling power, where divine interposition is clearly exerted (if we allow it ever to be exerted at all), it follows that Shakespeare, in representing the lives of the greatest and best of human beings as the sport of *chance,* does literally follow the order of God and nature. *He* is bitter, and *we* are bitter at this state of things, because we find it hard to realize the truth, that it is neither a man's worldly fortunes, nor the adherence of his friends, nor the fidelity of his wife, nor the time, nor the manner of his death, but the *tenor of his life,* which determines whether he be properly an object of envy or of pity. Humanly speaking, what is there more horrible, or more unjust in Shakespeare, than that a good man, after a life of mortification and obedience to his Maker's will, should be secretly murdered in a dungeon at the pleasure of a light dancer? The wicked "*have done to him what they listed!*" Had this been narrated merely in a novel or a play, the author's morality had doubtless been questioned, and he had been accused of setting an injurious example. All other means failing, better have introduced an angel to burst the prison door, than that this should have been. But God teaches otherwise. *He* leaves his faithful servant to perish, *if this be to perish.* And because it *is* God who thus acts and teaches, mankind, whether good or bad, are not hereby offended. With the former it is, "Though he slay me, yet will I trust in him." With the latter, "Let me die the death of the righteous, and let my last end be like his." So long as any hope remains, this will ever be the wish of the human heart.

Mr. Ruskin thinks that it was necessary for Shakespeare's special work "that he should be put, as it were, on a level with his race, on those plains of Stratford." True; and it was equally necessary that he should be so placed at that particular time, when the Reformation had excited in men's minds great curiosity concerning the Scriptures, which had been a sealed book to them. We have given much evidence that Shakespeare must have shared and gratified this curiosity—for hence his genius imbibed and assimilated that wisdom whereat the world marvels.

THE END.

SHAKESPEARE AND THE BIBLE. By the Rev. T. R. EATON. Giving Parallel Passages from the Plays of Shakespeare and the Bible, showing Where and How the Great Dramatist was indebted to Holy Writ for his Wisdom and Profound Knowledge of Human Nature. Crown 8vo., cloth, price 5s.

"Less is said to be known of Shakespeare than of any other writer who attained equal celebrity during his lifetime. This may be partly owing to the absence of that periodical literature which is now the rapid vehicle of information, and partly to his calling, and the nature of his great works, which, however well adapted for the closet, were originally designed for the stage. . . . . The reformation could not fail, from the very nature of it, to tinge the literature of the Elizabethan era. It gave a logical and disputatious character to the age, and produced men mighty in the Scriptures."—*Introduction.*

"Occasionally the coincidences are detected with considerable acumen, and the dramatist is traced to a Scriptural source with much ingenuity. The best part of the book is towards the conclusion, where the general resemblance between the inspired writers and Shakespeare is pointed out. Here is a fair ground of comparison, and it is giving to the mighty dramatist his highest due thus exultingly to compare him."—*Critic.*

"Subtle and lucky parallelisms; the book deserves to occupy a few pages of the next edition of Shakspeare. Mr. Eaton's elaborate comparison of the stories of Macbeth and Ahab deserve praise. He shows that, as the Bible, Shakspeare associates light with good, darkness with evil; that he describes men as born with unchangeable natures, sheep and goats, wolves and lambs. He, not without justice, shows scripture influence in the idea of Hamlet's ghost, and in the solemnity and frequency with which the poet alludes to the parable of Dives and Lazarus."—*Athenæum.*

"This is, we believe, the first time that an attempt has been regularly and systematically made to bring out the actual scripture passages to which Shakespeare has alluded, and, therefore, Mr. Eaton has to be congratulated for the manner in which he has treated such a subject."—*Bell's Messenger.*

"The reader will find classed together a very remarkable array of passages, references, and allusions, not often observed in this light, but whose accumulative force is great, and justifies our author's theory. This collection of parallel passages has a curious effect, and will give even the oldest Shakesperian a new view of the mind, and powers and training of our greatest bard."—*Birmingham Journal.*

LONDON: JAMES BLACKWOOD, Paternoster Row

LEAVES FROM THE BOOK OF NATURE. By M. S. DE VERE. With Preface by THOMAS DICK, LL.D., F.R.A.S., Author of the "Christian Philosopher," "Celestial Scenery," &c. Numerous Illustrations. Fcap. 8vo., cloth, 3s. 6d.; gilt edges, 4s.

CONTENTS.

ONLY A PEBBLE	LATER YEARS OF A PLANT
NATURE IN MOTION	PLANT MUMMIES
THE OCEAN AND ITS LIFE	UNKNOWN TONGUES
A CHAT ABOUT PLANTS	A TRIP TO THE MOON
YOUNGER YEARS OF A PLANT	

"A rich store of facts, with abundance of curious and interesting illustrations, displaying knowledge, ability, and good taste, in no ordinary degree."—*Leader.*

"An immense number of facts are detailed, not generally known to the common reader. I advise the reader to add it to his library, to which it will form a most useful addition. It is beautifully got up, and would form an excellent class-book in a school."—*Galway Mercury.*

"We here present our countrymen with a very useful and interesting work. The author shows himself to be intimately acquainted with the scenery of nature, especially as exhibited in our terrestrial system. In his chapter entitled 'Nature in Motion,' he depicts, in a very striking and interesting manner, the numerous motions which are going forward on the surface of our globe—the earth itself in its annual and diurnal movements—the rocks which, in one shape or another, are continually shifting their position, and rolling towards the ocean—the ocean itself in its tides and currents—volcanoes and earthquakes—glaciers—islands rising above the surface of the ocean—the sea overflowing lands, and retiring from them—the migrations of birds, fishes, insects, and vegetables, &c., &c.:—on these and numerous other topics, an immense number of curious facts are detailed, not generally known to the common reader. The same thing may be said with regard to his chapters on Plants, which contain an immense variety of curious and entertaining facts, anecdotes, and descriptions of various kinds, which cannot fail highly to gratify every reader. The author appears to be intimately acquainted with geology, zoology, botany, geography, and other sciences connected with natural history. He writes with great spirit and elegance, and with a considerable degree of humour. The work is written in the spirit of a true Christian philosopher, and he takes every opportunity of adverting to the evidences of Divine beneficence and wisdom which appear in the works of the Creator. It must have cost him immense labour and research in order to become acquainted with all the facts which are detailed in this interesting volume, which cannot fail to gratify and entertain the British reader."—*Dr. Dick.*

THE SACRED PLAINS. By J. H. HEADLEY. 18mo., cloth, price 1s. 6d.; or gilt edges, 2s.

CONTENTS.

The Plains of Shinar	The Plains of Shiloh
The Plains of Jordan	The Plains of Moreh
The Plains of Mamre	The Plains of Dura
The Plains of Moab	The Plains of Esdraelon
The Plains of Jericho	The Plain of Damascus
The Plains of Sharon	The Plains of Galilee

"The design of the following work, like that of its precursor (the Sacred Mountains), is to render more familiar and life-like some of the scenes commemorated in the Bible. The Bible, like the great fountain of boundless love it commemorates, is inexhaustible, and every attempt to arrange its scenes, define its localities, and elucidate its truths, is not only commendable in itself, but of paramount importance to the Bible student, whose mind wishes to obtain clear and distinct ideas of certain localities, and the events connected with them. Hence I have thought the Sacred Plains worthy of a separate niche in the Christian mind. If they do not tower aloft with that sublime and awful majesty with which the mountains are invested, they are nevertheless connected with some of the most interesting and stirring events recorded in the Bible, and to elucidate them clearly and distinctly has been one of my chief objects. I have, throughout the work, endeavoured to connect one leading incident with each locality, which I have amplified. Other minor incidents I have treated somewhat briefly, or made them subservient to the leading picture. The Bible and a map of Palestine have been my only text-books."—*Preface.*

London: JAMES BLACKWOOD, Paternoster Row.

LUTHER; or, Rome and the Reformation. By the Rev. R. MONTGOMERY, M.A. Sixth Edition. 8vo., Cloth, 5s.

"We think this work the least blemished and the most poetical he has given to the public. It is impossible to deny it the praise of containing right and noble sentiments, sometimes finely expressed, and disclosing poet-feeling."—*Nonconformist.*

"That portion of Mr. Montgomery's work which has reference to the Jesuits contains many passages of extraordinary power and beauty—a work in which the character of the great Reformer is developed with no common power, and which, while it exposes with uncompromising fidelity the errors of popery, clearly sets forth and eloquently enforces those fundamental doctrines of the Gospel, the hearty and practical reception of which constitutes the very essence of practical Christianity."—*Englishwoman's Magazine.*

"It is of great worth; the diction is vivacious, rich, perspicuous, and often exceedingly felicitous. The work is thoroughly Protestant and evangelical, and hence an admirable and seasonable antidote to popery. We hope it will have an extensive circulation."—*Wesley Banner.*

"This poem is entitled to no mean rank as a poetical composition. It contains passages of great power and pathos, and is sustained by large and scriptural views."—*Evangelical Magazine.*

"He (the author) possesses a most felicitous ear for rhythm, an extraordinary command of poetic diction, and a power, it would seem, of rapid composition, of very rare occurrence."—*British Quarterly.*

"His (Montgomery's) poetry represents many of the most familiar, and at the same time the most healthful, tendencies of the English national mind. 'Luther' is replete with vigorous reasoning, and characterized by what we may call a certain point of beauty, and a stately magnificence of verse in those passages in which the beauties of nature are portrayed, or the faith and honour of the great Redeemer are vindicated."—*English Review.*

"No poetic work has ever been more enthusiastically welcomed than this. That the present is a SIXTH edition speaks emphatically enough for its popularity. It is quite plain, indeed, looking merely to its commanding circulation, that 'Luther' is addressed to faculties higher than the merely æsthetic, and has appealed to those grand and abiding sympathies of intellect and heart which submit neither to the vicissitudes of taste nor the caprice of fashion. We need scarcely say, in bringing this notice to a close, how cordially at this particular juncture we welcome this new and extended edition of 'Luther.'"—*Dublin Warder.*

"In point of thought, energy of diction, and stability of structure, a more elaborate or more noble poem has scarcely ever been constructed."—*Bell's Messenger.*

"He has treated the subject with considerable poetic power both of thought and expression. The structure of the work is novel, admitting of any degree of expansion, and the author in the course of his narrative has taken occasion to introduce full and clear expositions of the leading doctrines of Christianity. 'The Poet's Retrospect and Patriot's Conclusion' comprises a fine evolution of thought, accompanied by an outburst of patriotic and devotional feeling expressed in passages of great poetic beauty."—*Norfolk Chronicle.*

"'Luther; or, Rome and the Reformation,' is decidedly the best of his poems of any considerable length. The fact that it has already reached the sixth edition is proof of its merit. . . . It is an excellent book for the drawing-room."—*Edinburgh Witness.*

THE IDOL DEMOLISHED BY ITS OWN PRIEST: An Answer to Cardinal Wiseman's Lectures on Transubstantiation. By JAMES SHERIDAN KNOWLES. Second Thousand. Small 8vo., cloth, price 3s. 6d.

"He has written with great vigour and power, and assailed Catholicism in its vulnerable points with a vigour and power but seldom equalled. Some of Mr. Knowles's arguments are new, and in dealing with the mass he has brought forward principles of interpretation on the whole correct, but which have hitherto been overlooked, and which bear strongly against the doctrine of Transubstantiation. We commend the book to readers of all classes."—*Glasgow Examiner.*

"The truly excellent and masterly style in which he overthrows the sophistry contained in the Cardinal's Lectures will be admired by every Protestant who may be fortunate enough to peruse the work."—*Cambridge Independent Press.*

"His (Dr. Wiseman's) sophistry, unfairness, and shameful mutilation of holy Scripture, are duly shown up in Mr. Knowles's pages."—*Methodist Magazine.*

London: JAMES BLACKWOOD, Paternoster Row.

A CHRISTMAS, THE NEXT CHRISTMAS, AND THE CHRISTMAS AFTER THAT: a Tale in Three Tellings. By THEOPHILUS OPER. Small 8vo., price 2s. 6d.

LORIMER LITTLEGOOD, Esq., a Young Gentleman who wished to see Society, and saw it accordingly. By ALFRED W. COLE, Esq., Barrister. With numerous Illustrations by Cruickshank and M'Connell. 8vo. cloth, price 10s. 6d.

" The opening of the tale promises well."—*Sheffield Free Press.*

" It will prove a very amusing volume. Well written."—*Cheltenham Chronicle.*

" Deserving of a place in our libraries, and the perusal of which on some dull forenoon or wet evening will yield pleasure not unmixed with profit."

" We are convinced, from the dramatic element, and the artistic grouping and contrast of character displayed in what we have seen of it, that it will in no way lack interest. The writing is quaint, humorous, graphic. If the reader wishes to take a peep at London life as it is, if he cares to see himself in a faithful mirror, if he would extend his sympathies more widely, if he would learn more of truth, which can alone he derived from human experience, he would not defeat any of these objects by reading ' Lorimer Littlegood.' "—*Glasgow Citizen.*

" The tale bids fair to be interesting."—*Monthly Register.*

" A very good tale very well told; there is much graphic, powerful, and occasionally humorous writing in it."—*Bath Journal.*

" Highly entertaining."—*Cheltenham Chronicle.*

" Written in a pleasing, lively, and terse style."—*Brighton Gazette.*

" Several really good incidents. The tale generally becomes more and more engrossing."—*Brighton Gazette.*

" The narration will he found highly interesting by all lovers of humorous ideas. . . . A very readable novel."—*Monthly Register.*

" Will afford a good deal of amusement."—*Edinburgh Courant.*

DOGS: their Sagacity, Instinct, and Uses; with Descriptions of their several Varieties. By GEORGE FREDERICK PARDON. With Drawings of upwards of Thirty Dogs, by HARRISON WEIR. Fcap. cloth, 3s. 6d.; gilt edges 4s.

CONTENTS.

Introduction—About Dogs in General—The History and Zoological Classification of the Dog—Various Kinds of Wild Dogs—The Greyhound—The Deerhound, the Wolf-dog, etc.—The Spaniel—The Newfoundland Dog—The Water Spaniel—The Shepherd's Dog and the Drover's Dog—The Esquimaux and the Lapland Dog—The Poodle, the Barbet, and the Cur—King Charles's Spaniels—The Staghound and the Talbot—The Foxhound—The Bloodhound—The Setter and the Pointer—The Harrier, the Otter-Hound, and the Beagle—The Mastiff, the Bulldog, and the Bull-Terrier—The English Terrier—The Scotch Terrier, the Shock-Dog, and the Turnspit—Instinct in Dogs—Miscellaneous Anecdotes of Dogs.

" Of all creatures, the dog alone seems capable of ministering to our wants without servility, of receiving reproof without complaint, of displaying for both rich and poor an equal ardour of friendship, and of following us to our graves with real and unselfish regret. In nearly all parts of the world the dog is the servant and friend of man; a collection of anecdotes, therefore, concerning this faithful animal cannot but prove interesting."—*Preface.*

London: JAMES BLACKWOOD, Paternoster Row.

TRAVELS AMONG ALPINE SCENERY. By Dr. CHEEVER and J. T. HEADLEY. With six Illustrations.

> " Ye living flowers that skirt the eternal frost!
> Ye wild goats sporting round the eagle's nest!
> Ye eagles, playmates of the mountain storm!
> Ye lightninge, the dread arrows of the clouds!
> Ye signs and wonders of the elements!
> Utter forth GOD! and fill the hills with praise!"—*Coleridge.*

" Too much cannot be written on the grand and sublime in nature; it tends to elevate the mind and enlarge our conceptions of the greatness and eternity of the Almighty, as well as to encourage reflection and improve the heart."—*Preface.*

PERSONAL ADVENTURES IN SOUTH AFRICA. By the Rev. G. BROWN, Graaff Reinet, Cape of Good Hope. With six Illustrations.

" I well remember the deep interest that was taken in the native races of South Africa in those religious circles in which it was my happiness to mingle before I left my native land, and know the feelings that are cherished by the pious and benevolent there in reference to especially the Caffre tribes here. Then I too cherished all those same feelings, and came gradually to an entire change of my views and feelings only after I had seen things here with my own eyes."—*Preface.*

BELIEVER'S JOURNEY (THE); and Future Home in the Better Land. By the Rev. A. C. THOMPSON. Preface by the Rev. Dr. ARCHER.

CONTENTS.

I. The Pilgrimage
II. Clusters of Eshcol
III. Waymarks
IV. Glimpses of the Land
V. The Passage
VI. The Recognition of Friends
VII. The Heavenly Banquet
VIII. Children in Heaven
IX. Society of Angels
X. Society of the Saviour
XI. Heavenly Honour and Riches
XII. No Tears in Heaven
XIII. Holiness of Heaven
XIV. Activity of Heaven
XV. Resurrection Body
XVI. Perpetuity in Heaven

" The idea of the work is a scriptural one; the method is excellent, the writing is no less so; the style is remarkably good, being at once forcible and figurative, rich in illustration—historical, poetical, and theological. The chapter on 'Children in Heaven' is worthy of particular notice. We conclude by cordially recommending this volume to all."—*Scottish Guardian.*

" The writer is in the succession of the glorious dreamer of Bedford, and very worthily does he sustain his lineage; his style is pictorial, and everywhere full of meaning, and not seldom suggestive of important thought. . . . . While the author is thoroughly sound, he is captivating, instructive, and stimulating."—*Christian Witness.*

" The style is poetical and the sentiment unctuous, well adapted to the tastes of the large number of readers."—*Clerical Journal.*

" It deserves high commendation, and will, I trust, be extensively read, and much blessed of God."—*Rev. R. Macdonald.*

" What noble and attractive themes! and Mr. Thompson discusses them with a clear intellect, a chaste yet glowing style, and a fervid, almost overflowing, heart."—*Christian Herald.*

London: JAMES BLACKWOOD, Paternoster Row.

ELEGANT AND ILLUSTRATED
BOOKS FOR YOUNG PERSONS.

PARLOUR PASTIMES; containing all the popular Fireside Games, Riddles, Natural Magic, Charades, &c., &c. 16mo, full gilt back, side, and edges. Illustrated. 3s. 6d.

"This is a delightful book for the young, and calculated to render home happy."

It is not necessary to enter into any kind of explanation or apology for a book of this description. Every parent knows that children want amusement at home; and to provide that amusement—innocent, harmless, and easy of attainment—has been the aim of the projectors of this little book. Among its contents will be found many old friends with new faces, as well as much that is entirely original. These PARLOUR PASTIMES serve, indeed, a higher purpose than mere amusement. They stimulate the faculties, arouse the wit, and, under the guise of amusement, develop and exercise the mental functions. Nor is this all: they foster harmony and unity of feeling; and, by community of pleasure, cultivate love, sympathy, and good-fellowship in youthful hearts."—*Preface.*

This work contains Acting Charades—Pantomime Charades—Dialogue Charades—86 Fireside Games—10 Enigmas—8 Charades, —4 Logogriphs—8 Arithmetical Puzzles—11 Mechanical Puzzles —Conundrums—Transpositions—Anagrams—Parlour Magic, &c., &c.

GAMES FOR ALL SEASONS; a Sequel to Parlour Pastimes. 16mo, full gilt back, side, and edges. Price 3s. 6d.

This work is a companion to the Parlour Pastimes, and contains all the Popular Out-door Games, Athletic Exercises, Amusements, Sports. No little library can be complete without it.

THE FROST KING; or, The Power of Kindness, and how it Prevailed over Fear and Cruelty. Numerous Illustrations, Imperial 16mo, full gilt back, side, and edges. Price 3s. 6d.

CONTENTS.

The Frost King; or, The Power of Kindness	Little Annie's Dream
Eva's Visit to Fairy Land	Star-Twinkle; or, The Flowers' Lesson on Humility
Lily-Bell and Thistle-Down	The May-Day Festival
Little Bud	The Voice of the Wind
Little Sunbeam's Song of Clover Blossom	Ripple, the Water-Spirit
	Fairy Song

NATURAL HISTORY (The) OF SELBORNE, with Observations on various parts of Nature; and the Naturalist's Calendar. By the late Rev. G. WHITE, A.M.; with extensive additions, by CAPTAIN THOMAS BROWN, F.L.S. Eleventh Edition, with nearly 40 Illustrations. Fcap. cloth, gilt back. Price 3s.; or gilt edges, 3s. 6d.

"The minute exactness of his facts—the good taste displayed in their selection—and the elegance and liveliness with which they are described—render this one of the most amusing books of the kind ever published, and it has gained for the author a high and just reputation."—*Preface.*

London: JAMES BLACKWOOD, Paternoster Row.

www.ingramcontent.com/pod-product-compliance
Lightning Source LLC
Chambersburg PA
CBHW021825230426
43669CB00008B/869